# BROWN FACES GO WHITE

## ESSAYS ON POPULAR CULTURE OF TAMIL NADU

R KUMARAN

Made with ♥ on the Notion Press Platform
www.notionpress.com

*For my parents,*

*Who, even in their benign ignorance of what I had been doing, stood by me throughout!*

# Contents

# Preface

Tamil films, which have been understood in different manners by different scholars as an industry as a "Folk Culture" and as a "Cultural Medium," have attracted the curiosity of the scholars (both from within India and without) who are interested in understanding Indian society in general and Tamil society in particular. Even though films in India occupy a special place evoking scholarly attention, their place in Tamil society is unique and has been fairly documented.

The uniqueness of Tamil films has been analyzed from various angles; from the point of view their political significance (Hardgrave 1979); from the viewpoint of the personality cults the films encouraged (M.S.S. Pandian 1992 and M.Kennedy 1992); from the perspective of how the audience participates in and understands the culture of Tamil films (Sara Dickey 1993).

Although all these studies have thrown enough light on various aspects of Tamil Films and their link with Dravidian politics, they have failed to connect Tamil films to Dravidian movement's politics of culture. While they have paid serious attention to the culture of Dravidian movement's politics, they have left the politics of culture of Dravidian movement largely unexplored. Thanks to this, the process of culture construction initiated and sustained by Dravidian movement remains to be interrogated. Secondly, they have failed to locate the heroes of Tamil films in the backdrop of the cultural idioms and codes generated by the same process of culture construction. And thirdly and more importantly, these studies, in the process of analyzing the individual cases, have largely failed to grasp the concept of person discernible in the dominant cultural medium of Tamil society viz., films.

The study elaborated in this book, seeks to take due cognizance of these inadequacies in the existing studies and will try to put forth correctives to them. The main purpose of my study would be to analyze and understand the shift that is perceptible in the way personhood in Tamil films has been conceptualized. Thus, this study would try to account for the dramatic movement away from the way the concept of person was shown in Tamil films till recently to a surprisingly new way of deploying the concept of person as observable in the new spate of Tamil movies that have come out in the last three or four years. Whereas the old concept of person as seen through Tamil films, strictly adhered to the idioms and codes generated by Dravidian movement, the defining concept of person breaks and violates these idioms and codes and presents a completely new person, whose significance, especially in the context of socio-economic-political changes of the recent period, would be the focus of my study. The study assumes that the continuum against which M.G.R., Rajnikanth and other Tamil actors were seen as mere extensions, is being broken.

Let me introduce a caveat here. The problem besetting film studies in general is the privileging of the analyst's reading of the filmic text, by submitting the film narrative to certain ideological and political analysis which obliterates the real people from the analytical framework. Thus, it fails to fully understand the way the masses perceive and make sense of the filmic text. This, I understand, arises out of lack of phenomenological sensitivity on the part of researchers. By investing the popular consciousness with knowledgeability and creative imagination, I propose to privilege the popular perception over the researcher's self-privileged perception. This entails an understanding of how popular consciousness interacts with cultural media and the various ideological processes mediated therein. Against the deterministic view that cultural media constitute social perception and identity, I hypothesize that popular consciousness is not a passive recipient; instead it builds its own repertory of resistant and negotiatory mechanisms through which it constructs its own life world. I am confident that a study undertaken with the above perspective would help us appreciate the resilient character of popular culture and as to how it responds to the newly emerging social realities. The study also furthers the argument that culture in general and popular culture in particular acts as a site on the terrain of which the negotiation with new realties take place and as a medium through which the same pass out as less-shocking and acceptable. In other words, popular culture neutralizes the shock-value of unfamiliar and new.

# Acknowledgements

When I was writing this book, I fantasized about this moment. As the signal of end of a long project, the time for acknowledgments seemed like an impossible dream. However, now that I am here, I find myself stymied in my wish to remember with grace and gratitude all those who have helped me along the long and meandering route of this research work.

Any research work is a collective product drawing on our interactions with others. I do admit that I have no way of adequately acknowledging the contributions of all those who helped me in the completion and finalizing of this research project. However, I would like to mention some, without whose help this dissertation could not have been completed.

I would like to begin by thanking Dr.Roma Chatterji who has been supportive whenever unself-assuredness crept into me. Her patient and sympathetic attitude has helped enormously in finalizing the draft of my dissertation. I would particularly like to thank her for her intellectual companionship and for her directness of her criticisms, which she always managed to couch in the most no-nonsense terms. I would also like express my deep gratitude to other faculty members, among whom Dr.Deepak Mehta deserves special mention, for their help throughout my M.Phil. course. Those of my friends who bore with my occasional intellectual ramblings into film theory and techniques also merit mention here. More specifically I must thank Ajay Verma and Rizwan Ahmad.

In my pre-UGC- fellowship days, when things were going really tough, Thiru Sankaran Appa and Y.S.Lee had generously helped me. Without their ever-willing benediction, I could not have hoped to reach this stage, my heartfelt thanks are due to them.

I am beholden also to Mr.A.K.Joshi, who stoically bore with my repeated and successive demands for alteration and amendments when typing this dissertation. My thanks to his family members for they received me with warmth and hospitality whenever I visited them for resuming the typing works. My friend M.Prashant's assistance in this regard needs special mention. I thank him profusely.

I would like to end by thanking my family members, who for the first time ever in their lives, were faced with tremendous difficulty reconciling to my continued absence from my home during my student days in Delhi.

*R.Kumaran*

CHAPTER ONE

# AN OVERVIEW

Tamil films, which have been understood in different ways as an industry as a folk cultural form and as a cultural medium, - have attracted the curiosity of the scholars (both from within India and without), who are interested in understanding Indian society in general and Tamil society in particular. Even though films occupy a special place in the scholarship of India, their place in Tamil society is unique and has been fairly well documented. The uniqueness of Tamil films has been analyzed from various angles; from the point of view of theirs political significance (Hardgrave, 1979); from the view point of the personality cults the films encouraged (MSS Pandian 1992 and M.Kennedy 1992); and from the perspective of how the audiences participate in and understand the culture of Tamil films (Sara Dickey 1993)

Robert Hardgrave and Sara Dickey in their brief analyses of the cinema-sponsored political culture of Tamil society (Hardgrave 1979: 46-52, Sara Dickey 1990) have looked into the way in which the individual members of Tamil society respond to the personality of cine stars, of whom some are potential and others, actual politicians. Hardgrave's highly empirical analysis explores the film-going behaviour of the Tamils and their assessment of cine stars as brother, as teacher (Vathiyar as MGR Was fondly called), as leader (Thalaivair) and as demigods. Hardgrave attributes the sentimentalized politics in Tamil Nadu to the "infantile" nature of democratic politics (Hardgrave Jr. 1979:52). In his view the late arrival of electoral politics in Tamil Nadu did not meet with success, as the pre-conditions for the flourishing of democratic politics were largely absent. Arguing almost on similar lines, Sara Dickey makes an inventory of the kind of activities, which the fan clubs of various films actors are involved in. Her focus is specifically on the fan clubs which function not only to ensure the success of their favourite film actors, but also as reservoir of cadets and vote-bank, if and when the particular films actors happen to be politicians (Dickey 1992: 422). They may also function as profit-making economic units by organizing film shows (Dickey 1992: 423). Both studies are highly descriptive and offer little in the form of analysis of film as an audio-visual medium. They are more interested in the political culture of Tamil society, and they make no attempt to study the nature of response to film-culture within Tamil cultural system in general and worldview of Tamils in particular. A genuine culturological approach would well behoove us to tease out the cultural categories concerning the notion of person, hero and so on, and then connect them to the uniqueness of political culture. Their studies also miss out on the essential connection between the cultural and political realms, because their studies have a glaringly broad perspective, trying to describe everything in the name of political culture. They could have arrived at more valid conclusions, if they had singled out film as a visual medium, which is an entry-point into the contemporary Tamil political history.

Kathirkesu Sivathambi in his booklet 'Cinema as a Medium for Political Communication', avoids the pitfalls into which the above-mentioned studies have been trapped. In a brief but incisive analysis of the way in which political parties and their leaders propagate their ideals and principles, Sivathambi throws light on how films just took off from where other cultural forms such as drama etc., were left off. He also illuminates on the themes and songs, which were tailor-made to suit the Dravidian political party during 1950's and 60's (Sivathambi, 1984). Here again one may notice the lack of a proper analytical framework that would have captured the elusive connections between culture and politics. Although mention is made of other popular cultural traditions from which cinema benefited in defining itself in the Tamil context, the question as to why it should succeed in Tamil society alone remains unexplored. Yet, this criticism should not be taken as a plea for discovering the causative agent to explain the unique political situation in Tamil Nadu.

M.S.S.Pandian in his highly polemical work (polemical in that it is highly critical of AIADMK's politics headed by M.G.Ramachandran, the film actor-turned Politician) on the personality cult surrounding the famous film actor MGR, attempts to explain the reasons for the popularity of MGR (Pandian, 1992). This is a personality-specific study in the sense that only MGR phenomenon is being analyzed in his book. This may obliquely function as an apology for exonerating Tamils from the passivity, which has been assigned to them by earlier studies. The rationale for MGR's popularity is traced to a certain cultural phenomenon namely folk-hero worship, which is found in various parts of Tamil Nadu. (Pandian, 1992: 18) MGR is a pan-Tamil folk-hero as his phenomenon is continuum of folk-hero worship practised across Tamil Nadu (Pandian 1992:22). In the latter case also the folk-heroes by their extraordinary feats have become divine beings. Here, Pandian probes into the popular consciousness of Tamils and arrives at an interesting but less convincing explanation for the stupendous popularity that MGR enjoyed. His work is certainly an improvement on the earlier works. Yet, it makes certain convenient but controversial connections between the higher rate of popularity of MGR with the rural masses on the one hand, and treating the electoral success of MGR, as an index for his all-powerful popularity across the entire Tamil society on the other. Being an attempt in the historical sociology, it perhaps fails to locate MGR's persona in the larger ambit of the concept of person which shows a remarkable continuity with, of course, the inherent dynamism and perceptible vicissitudes. Singling out the MGR phenomenon for the purpose of analysis does grave injustice to the counterpoising trends, which are contemporaneous to the MGR phenomenon. Moreover, it cannot be presumed that MGR's handling of his image as pure, saintly, do-gooder always succeeded, as this would be equivalent to causing violence to the numerous audiences who watch MGR films for different reasons, sometimes to just confirm their dislike for MGR. No image of icon enjoys consensual approval from the followers, nor does it function as a singular medium for articulating the aspiration of a particular group. The exceptionality of the public icons is that they are apparently autogenous and actually unownable (or owned-by- all, depending upon where it is looked at from). Particularly in a social context like Tamil Nadu, wherein competing caste groups and classes are staking a moral claim over public images and icons, how images of actors and other figures are subject to multiple contestation by competing groups, need also to be analyzed. Fred Clothey's study of the image of a Tamil God comes as refreshing corrective here. Clothey's understanding of Lord Murugan corroborates the public character of the images and how there is a continuing contest over making them coextensive with the aspiration of competing groups. (Fred Clothey, 1978:4)

Arguing that the image of Lord Murugan has been used to symbolically resolve the paradoxes arising out of the changing aspiration of Tamils whose evanescent provincialism has to jell well with the nascent Indian nationalism (Ibid; 1978: 4), Clothey makes a case for the necessity to strike congruence between the mood of the contemporary Tamil Nadu and the corresponding modification in the contours of the image of God (Ibid). In the light of Clothey's analysis, the lacunae in M.S.S.Pandian's work become much more evident. Accepting the fact that the phenomenal popularity of MGR hinged upon the pre-existing forms of folk-hero worship, one should not declare the issue settled, for as argued by Pandian there is no neat-fit between a contemporary image and the ancient form of worship. There are certain intermediating tendencies, which preclude a one-to-one correlation between these two orders. This style of argument is tantamount to wrenching out these two events out of their socio-politico-existential context. This is attested by the fact that those cine-actors who aped MGR's mannerisms could not succeed on a large-scale. Thus, a valid and rigorous understanding of the genealogy of an image cannot remain oblivious to the changing aspiration- structure of the social actors.

For the important reason that the alteration in the aspiration-structure creates painful and disequilibrating rupture and tension with the preexisting, established and fairly entrenched values and normative order of a given society, there should be a symbolic resolution of that tension, so that real action in the social terrain becomes possible. Hence, symbols assume enormous importance here, for it is through the repertoire of symbols, icons and images, that the paradoxes are resolved. If the popularization of Lord Murugan was the consummation of the process of the successful resolution of paradox entailed by conflicting imagination of Tamil as a nation and the emerging pan-Indian national consciousness, then MGR's image is equally pregnant with similar symbolic potency to mediate some other aspiration of Tamil community. And this aspect is yet to be interrogated thoroughly. An attempt along that line is needed, so that one can arrive at a better understanding of the dynamics operating behind the construction of the image of Tamil person, rather than the image of personalities, It is only in the above mode that one can abstract the dominant cultural notion of person, which can be situated at the inter-section of cultural, social and political processes current in Tamil society.

It may be instructive to consider what Sara Dickey in her later book on Tamil cinema has to say about the interface between the mood and art medium that is cinema. Unlike the articles mentioned above, this book focuses its attention on cinema and as to how the urban poor in Tamil Nadu relate to it (Dickey 1993). Eschewing the usual concerns evinced by other scholars in their understanding of personality cult in Tamil Nadu, she concentrates rather on how film-going as a social activity tends to have far-reaching impact and implication for the urban poor in making sense of their life-situations (Dickey 1993: 17). She also argues that popular films in Tamil Nadu, by extolling the virtues of poor, come close to the lives of poor (Dickey 1992: 17). In keeping with Victor Turner's performance theory, she suggests that these films are also commentaries on the larger social currents. As an anthropological exercise her study concerns itself more with the context than with the text. Although she undertakes textual analysis in her study, it is limited only to the interpretation of theme and plot of few select films rather than a proper interpretation of the audio-visual dimensions of the film. This criticism is applicable to almost all the studies reviewed above. A proper analysis of films, whenever they become central to our understanding of social phenomenon ought to take due cognizance of the audio-visual facets of the films, for these are the medium specific qualities of the film. What is entailed in the above-mentioned studies can be arrived at by a close reading of the scripts and dialogues of the films concerned, even without seeing them on screen. It is instructive in this context to note Ravi Vasudevan's suggestion. He says that "film or any comparable representational activity is excrescence that lies on the surface of reality waiting to be peeled away or decoded in the drive to uncover the underlying and more important socio-political content". He is interested "in the way the audio-visual dimensions of cultural activity (like film) are constitutive of social perception of reality" (Vasudevan 1995:2809).

One important shortcoming of the script-based film-studies is that they fail to capture the image-related details that may prove more illuminative to the task in hand. When I say image-related details, I mean image in its dynamic aspects and movement, which is special only to cinema. In this regard, it is helpful to note here Barthe's analysis of Eisenstein's ' Evan the terrible'. In spite of the image-specific interpretation, which Barthes undertakes, differing thus significantly from the script-based analysis of films, the quintessential quality of films, movement, is totally ignored by Barthes. This is to disagree with Barthes to whom, although image is important, it is the image in its stillness as it is available in the form of still photographs which functions as peepholes, opening into entire narrative structure of scene/film. (Barthes 1985). This inadvisable for (a) it obviates sound from the tapestry of film and (b) it violently brings film to a grinding halt for the sake of analysis. We can set aside Barthean plea for taking still photographs as the representation of scene/film as it arises out of an idealistic search for the 'Filmic' in cinema (Barthes 1985: 59-62).

Coming back to Sara Dickey's book on cinema and urban poor, it should be mentioned that it suffers from yet another lacuna i.e., the problem of a historicity. There is hardly a reference to the political history of Tamil society, which divided the film-going audience along party lines. Interestingly, it is only by a deep inspection of the political biography of the Tamil community that one can properly appreciate the positively evaluated relationship between Tamil audience and Tamil films. It goes without saying that it is thanks mainly to the unique unfolding of political history that films and other art forms have ensured audience and support for themselves. On the other hand, lack of appreciation of the socio-cultural history of Tamil society has handicapped Dickey in locating the set of films she has chosen for interpretation, in the precession of dynamic aspiration-structures of the collective Tamil psyche. The moment of arrival of a new set of films, if they show a dramatic difference vis-à-vis the antecedent tendencies, need to be contextualised. However, one must give credit go Dickey for undertaking case studies of select film-goers which reveal that the choice of films and film heroes coincide with their political ideologies. This is the first step in understanding as to how the jump from one set of actors to another occurs and the undercurrents beneath it.

Here one may again recall the work of Clothey, who traces the biography of Tamil God and metamorphoses it undergoes in consonance with the changing nature of Tamil self-consciousness. By juxtaposing the history of man in Tamil society along with changing face of Lord Murugan he could forge revealing connection between an image and Tamil's socio-cultural history, which subsumes the expanding horizon of Tamils self-consciousness. While Clothey could steer clear of the problem of competing interpretations of Lord Murugan by the multiple caste groups thanks to the unique nature of the image of Lord Murugan, (which becomes a consensual choice for all Tamils residing within and outside Tamil Nadu), the image of Tamil films heroes have been subject to multitudinal contestations and interpretations.

Anyhow not only does one have to possess a deeper understanding of contemporary history of Tamil Nadu, but also about the history of Tamil films. Theodore Baskaran's 'Message Bearers' (Baskaran 1981) comes handy in this respect. Surveying the history of Tamil films from its inception to 1945, Baskaran demonstrates the confluence of several folk-cultural forms with a modern medium like cinema. Yet, his work is not exclusively on films as it includes other entertainment media such as Drama, Popular songs, Gramophone etc. all of which however, telescope to form Tamil regional cinema (Baskaran 1981:xi). As he himself states, the history of Tamil cinema is traced through "the exigencies of the silent era, the convention of early talkies and repression of the British (because of all these) Tamil cinema was acquiring many of the characteristics that lasted beyond our period (Baskaran 1981: xi). There is an attempt made in this work to analyze the interrelationship between the social aspiration and its manifestation in entertainment forms (Baskaran 1981: 10). Baskaran notes "the themes opinions crusades of pop entertainment were bound to reflect the ideas and aspiration of a society in an era of historic change". (Baskaran 1981: xii). Nevertheless, this thesis is not pursued in great detail.

The interweaving of pan-Indian nationalist consciousness of Tamils with popular entertainment forms does not do justice to many dominant countercurrents prevalent in that era, for his work presents only one side of the cultural coin, as it were, of Tamil society. As a source book on the history of Tamil films in early era, this work proves to be extremely helpful. In yet another count, this is the first historiographical attempt, which looks sympathetically at the so-called 'low-cultural' forms as a vital database for understanding the history. An important limitation of this work is its time frame. The period covered that is 1888-1945, marks the beginning of consolidation of the discontent of non-Brahmin Tamils towards the entire project of Indian nationalists. Due to this there were vituperative attacks leveled against nationalist ambition, which were upheld by many pan-Indian nationalists in Tamil Nadu. The dissenting voice of the non-Brahmin Tamils began to articulate itself through cultural media including films, thereby forming a strong countertendency to Indian nationalist propaganda. Baskaran's construction of film-history makes no mention of these tendencies in his book. However, it is worth noting that the anti-nationalist forces had gained striking momentum and became dominant after independence till the Dravidian movement plunged into electoral politics. There is no such reference made in Baskaran's book.

One such instance in which one gets a clear exposition of how non-Brahmin sympathisers of the ideology of Dravidian Party identified themselves with the "Dravidian film" titled "Parasakthi" is narrated in elaborate detail by M.S.S.Pandian (Pandian 1991). Tracing the life and career of this film, Pandian throws light on the polarization among Tamils that 'Parasakthi' effected. While the Congress sympathizers demanded a ban on the screening of this film, for it allegedly incited anti-India feelings, the Dravidian Party supporters thronged cinema halls in large number to see this film. Here again, one clearly sees an overlaying of political ideologies on a filmic text (Pandian, 1991: 763). But what is manifestly absent in Pandian's work, like other works mentioned above, is a convincing and rigorous textual analysis and a formal narrative analysis of the given film(s) to demonstrate the process of impingement of political ideologies on the text. A text held purposefully against any given ideology stands amenable to the intrusion of the historian into its zone, and thus the texts are selectively constructed by historians to fit into the framework of historian's or sociologist's analysis. This problem has been dealt in great detail by Ravi Vasudevan (Vasudevan 1993). Particularly in those cases in which the ideological undercurrents are verified against the backdrop of the oral testimonies recorded in popular literature, one sees blatant imposition of historians' pre-judged assumptions on the narrative. Here, one may recall the work of Janice Radaway (Radaway, 1989) on the experience of woman readers of romantic fictions. Many of her conclusions regarding the formation of solidarity and the resultant subversion of patriarchal structures are not shared by the readers (Radaway, 1986).

Although overall blocking of the invasion of socio-historians may be difficult to achieve, a closer approximation of historical experience of audience with that of those enunciated in the text can be accomplished if such a reading of given text is executed in the light of specific socio-cultural notions governing the relationship between spectators and text. One of the vocal votaries for such a creative incorporation of notions of viewing cultural principles governing the act of perception and other notions is Ravi Vasudevan. Arguing for verifying the truth claims of the oral testimony not only in relation to the text and narrative but also to other extra-textual factors, he writes that in undertaking film studies in Indian context one (should) think of 'ways of seeing' organized by the temple, photo-deities, popular prints and movie posters" (Vasudevan, 1993: 53). Ravi Vasudevan pursues this thesis in a revealing analysis of two Hindi films of 1940's and 1950's (Vasudevan, 1993:1950). How the Hindu 'ways of seeing' is employed in portrayal of the hero and the 'look' he invites from the heroine is the subject of analysis (Vasudevan 1995). Here, one finds an interesting correspondence between the way we perceive divinity and that of heroines' perceiving of the hero. That such a portrayal is accompanied by bhajan only adds to the holiness created around the presence of the hero. Similar attempt is made for different reasons in another article by Vasudevan who explores the mode of representation and the narrative of family as specific to Indian cultural scene (Vasudevan 1993).

This is very important not only for the purpose of revealing the peculiarities specific to films in India in contrast to other homogenizing tendencies—Hollywood against Bombay social cinema or both put together against Tamil cinema—but also for capturing the rhythms of change that a society passes through. While the former becomes an exercise in carving out a space for national cinema against the onslaught of globalising forces, the latter throws light on the momentous change that a cultural form (like film) undergoes. A fruitful attempt in this respect can be made only when narrative analysis of film is not restricted within the porous wall of cultural system which is the limitation to some extent in Vasudevan's works—but situated alongside the processes initiated by political and economic changes.

Something closer to such and effort is made in Madhava Prasad's essay on the issue of 'kissing' in Indian popular cinema (Prasad 1993). Analyzing the prohibition of kissing scenes in popular Hindi films in relation to the notions of public versus private spheres and these two read against the western realistic understanding of films as doorway leading into the private psychic landscape of individual characters, Prasad concludes in a convincing manner as to how films in India are more of a public statements on the public lives of the character, hence the prohibition of kissing as it happens in the private realm of individuals. These conclusions are to be read in the light of the state-sponsored ideologies of family and Congress-defined socialism. Madhava Prasad sums up his conclusion this way "thus at the heart of film industry an informal injunction that goes to work to prohibit the representation unfolds: the prohibition of representations of the private; the prohibition of cinema (as Metz defines it); the prohibition, by extension of the open acknowledgement of the capitalist nature of the new nation-state. Where socialism was only invoked as ideology, and Congress socialism was no more than a protective shield for the development of indigenous capitalism, the emerging capitalist culture had to be disavowed, this disavowal being the only (negative) proof of the existence of socialism". (Prasad 1993: 81-82)

While both Vasudevan and Madhava Prasad make a defensible case for integration of extra-cinematic discourses into the analysis of narratives, alongside the oral testimonies of audiences, in both their works the audience's account of how they experienced film is marginalized, if not totally absent. Even when they are included, they only speak of those audience responses which are aired by those who are learned enough to be well versed with the notion of realism and other aesthetic principles governing filmmaking. For example, in his narration of the experience of modernity as it was mediated by Indian popular cinema, only those educated and knowledgeable members of the audience (in one case he quotes from a letter written by a physician) are analyzed. This is in no way to discredit the merits of their work. Ravi Vasudevan and Prasad have shown the right direction towards which future studies should proceed. There is a refreshing movement away from mere aesthetic-based approach to cinema which one encounters in the works of Rajadhayaksha, Anuradha Kapur and Geetha Kapur, to a social semiotic approach, in Vasudevan and Prasad's work. Through the changing aesthetic tradition, which obtains on the terrain of narrative and text, Vasudevan and Prasad have demonstrated that one can capture the changing dynamics of society. Yet, what convinces one the most is their awareness that films or any other representational activity for that matter is not just a mirror naively reflecting the social reality, but a product also of ideological inflections superimposing on cultural media.

This book will aspire to overcome the limitations, which the above-reviewed studies suffer from in one way or other. As argued above, attempts will be made to tease out the constitutive and culturally defined notions, which govern the popular consciousness in Tamil society and its members' perception of social reality.

Important among these notions are those concerning the idea of person, perception, spatial organization (both within the given cultural media or in the real social life), the ideology of motherhood, and chivalry, the notions governing the act of storytelling etc. The existing expressive traditions in Tamil culture provide fertile ground to glean out these notions. And they have been well documented. Here one may recall the works of Arjun Appadurai, (1991) Stuart Blackburn (1986), A.K.Ramanujan, (1986), Margaret Travick (1990), Friedelm Hardy (1983) and others. These notions dug out there from, will back our attempts to get closer to the experiences of Tamil audience in negotiating the changes unleased by politic-economic forces in recent years. This way the transformation in the social order effected by globalization and liberalization of Indian economy will be analyzed as to what extent it has altered the contours of the old aspiration-structure of the Tamil society and as to how this turbulence is absorbed through a symbolic resolution of the paradoxes on the cultural terrain.

One is instantly reminded of Carol Breckenridge's (ed) Volume titled "Orientalism and The Post-Colonial Predicament" (1994). In it she argues as to how colonial categories have divided the mental landscape of Indians into, inter alia, Aryan/Dravidian, oppositions. Regarding the colonial government policies and their role in the emergence of non-Brahmin politics in Tamil Nadu see Irschick's, (1969) work on the non-Brahmin movement, covering the period starting from 1916 to 1929; Baker's (1976) study of Tamil politics and Barnetts (1976) book on the cultural nationalism of Tamil political parties, notably the DMK.

CHAPTER TWO

# THE CULTURAL POLITICS OF TAMIL NADU

When one examines the contemporary history of Tamil Nadu, one can infer that Tamil identity as it obtains now in its present form is the by-product of a variety of processes of which the most important ones are "revivalism" and "classicalisation". In their drive to trace the origin of Tamil civilization to a hoary past, the non-Brahmin leaders of many revivalist movements in Tamil Nadu had aspired to connect present day practices and other idealized images with that of the ancient ones. They tried to establish the greatness and glory of Tamil civilization in the light of the images drawn out from the classical Tamil literary works. The current state of ruin, degeneration and enslaved nature of Tamil culture (which was allegedly caused by Aryan influences) was contraposed to the prosperity and grandeur of the ancient Tamil civilization. Taking cues from ancient literary works such as "Kalitthokai" 'Paripatal' 'Pattpattu' 'Tolkappiyam' Cilapathikaram Manimekalai, Akananuru and Purananuru, and also from later literary works inspired by them, a highly romanticized image of ancient Tamil's everyday life, polity, religion etc., was constructed. (Hart 1975: 41-42). As their aim was to provide proofs of the independence and purity of pre-Aryan Tamil culture, they had to posit a pure Tamil religion, Tamil God and Tamil language; when they incorporated distinctly modern ideals like inequality, fraternity humanism and rationality, efforts were made to trace their origins in Tamil antiquity too. The equal status that women enjoyed along with men and the cosmopolitan outlook of Tamil citizens in the ancient society were highlighted with the help of literary evidences. The whole arsenal of symbols and metaphors which these movements culled out from the ancient literary sources went on to play a crucial role in the politics of modern Tamil society. The crystallization and consolidation of singular Tamil consciousness and imagined unity are the outcome of the clever use of these symbols and metaphors by leaders of the Dravidian movement and political parties.

Case study research: definition and characteristics

Case study research is a qualitative research method that focuses on the in-depth examination of a specific case, which can be an individual, group, organisation, community, or event. Case study research aims to provide a comprehensive understanding of the studied phenomenon, including its context, complexities, and dynamics.

What happened alongside the process of classicalisation was the historicalisation of Tamil identity. In fact, these two are clearly interrelated phenomena, though classicalisation is one by which the historicalisation of ethnic identities takes place. The emergence of a unity of consciousness among the members of a given ethnic group necessitates a unified history, which every member share. Thus, a whole new historical memory must be built in retrospect. To accomplish this one must be situated in the process of history. This is tied to the recovery of a distinct past differentiating insider from outsider. Here discrete events and diverse sources must be conjoined together with the assistance of certain symbols, so that continuity in the sense of having a unique identity can be achieved. In Tamil society, some of the preeminent symbols through which Tamils managed to affirm their continuity through history are Tamilaham (Tamil home land), which refers to territory, Centhamil (Pure/classical Tamil) referring to substance and Lord Murugan. It must be cautioned that the phrase “revivalist movements” used here, though suggests the general orientation of many streams within the self-respect movement and its earlier version. The justice party, the Periyar-headed Dravidar Kazhagam (DK) shows remarkable difference in its treatment of past. The D.K. is not revivalist as it aims at a prospectively realizable Tamil nationhood. (see M.S.S.Pandian (1991b)

Through these symbols various periods starting from the mythical past to present, are strung together, thereby excavating a history completely dissociated from a so-called “bramanical” one. We will elaborate on these symbols in the later part of this chapter.

Yet Tamil identity thus constructed has not remained in the same state in the course of contemporary Indian history. It has lent itself to revision, redefinition and contestation whenever such reviews suited the interest of specific groups - caste or religious or political or when the collective articulation of the entire Tamil community found it necessary and politically profitable.

**Dramatisation of Tamil Identity**

The demonstration of an imagined unity among the members of an ethnic group cannot succeed in realizing its goals unless it is dramatized through cultural forms, both for an internal audience (the actual and imagined members) as well as for an eternal audience which includes those against whom the demonstration is carried out. It is in the process of the dramatization of collective identity that the symbols and cultural media through which they are communicated, acquire utmost significance. It is here culture meets politics, as argued by Cohen when he says, "The culture is continuously interpenetrated by the political and is thereby transformed into ideology... Meanwhile the political is expressed articulated and objectified in terms of cultural forms and performances". (Cohen 1974: 13-14)

In the case of Tamil Nadu, the socio-religious reform movements and their political outfits in their endeavour to achieve nationhood and selfhood for Tamils used every conceivable cultural forms and cultural media. Novels, Drama, Music and Films are just to name a few. Of these, cinema became the dominant medium in the Post-independent era. Here again, one can see the preponderance of classical symbols through which the political and social philosophies of these groups were expressed.

A careful analysis of the modes, metaphors and codes through which Tamil identity was dramatized in the past and in their transformed nature in present era, reveals the importance of classical Tamil literature in this project. They formed a virtual encyclopedia to which references were made whenever varying aspects of Tamil self-hood were sought to be determined. Tamil identity as it is expressed in the image of Tamil personhood therefore, is a compendium of metaphors, symbols and codes tempered by the political exigencies of their given contexts. Drawing again upon Cohen, we may argue that the construction of a highly crystallized selfhood or subjectivity is essential for a politically motivated group when it intends ensure a steady supply of followers of members. Since the elicitation of overall commitments from the members is necessary for the realization of the collective goal, the deployment of symbols becomes important. For it is capable of invoking the total emotional involvement of members (Cohen 1974: 15). Here the significance of the image of a culturally desirable personhood becomes the dominant mode as it has the potential to pull into its orbit all other mode of dramatization of ethnic identity.

The image of personhood functions here as the point of entry into the entire processes historicalistion of Tamil identity, for it is the pivot around which other modes coheres and from which they derive their symbolic and political efficacy. In this context it is instructive to note Paul Willies analysis of the manner in which a contesting culture expresses its aspiration through the body of the typologised image of personhood. He says that the expression of opposition, which also implies foregrounding of a politically constructed identity, is mediated through a form of a configuration of the visual, the bodily, the stylistics of movement and interaction of the personae of individual members (Willies 1975: 251).

**The Content of Tamilness**

We have argued above that the Tamil identity consists of historically created metaphors and symbols mined from classical literature. What are the dominant symbols and metaphors whose manifestations of the terrain of the body of the Tamil person are visible? Here we may mention three dominant symbols: (1) Tamilaham (Territory) (2) Centhamil, (3) Tamilthai (Tamil Mother).

These three symbols express themselves in different metaphors. They are:

1. Thai Kulam (The notion of mother-community)
2. Kadamai (duty and responsibility)
3. Iratham (Blood)
4. Karppu (Chastity)

We will try to elaborate on these six themes when we analyze the image Lord Murugan (the quintessential Tamil God) in the light of Clothey's interesting book 'Many faces of Murugan' (1978).

The cult of Lord Murugan presents an interesting case for understanding the history of Tamil's collective aspiration and concerns. The changing socioeconomic circumstances in the modern era have effected corresponding changes in the way Murugan is visualized now and also in the way the cult's popularity is declining, being replaced by more cosmopolitan and working-class oriented Ayyappa cult. The phenomenal popularity however, of Murugan cult in the past, particularly during intense anti-Brahmin struggle in Tamil Nadu, owes its cause of Tamil renaissance, (which itself is the spin-off of colonial rule) and also to the later developments resulting in the enormous political victory for the Dravidian parties. It is ironical that even against their proclaimed adherence to atheism and anti-religious stance, the leaders of the Dravidian party had declared time and again that Murugan is the God of Tamil (Clothey 1978: 116). Although the history of Lord Murugan is identified by these renaissance Tamil scholars to be as old as the history of Tamil society itself, it is only during the last one and half century that the revitalization of this Tamil God has shown tremendous intensity. In the periods proceeding that, the cult of Murugan was localized and unknown to the larger public. The sudden popularity of Murugan cult may be due to a variety of reasons. Clothey argues that there are several reasons, not the least of which is that God is riding the crest of Tamil self-consciousness which has come to new focus in the mind of many Tamilians, at least since the publication of a comparative Dravidian grammar in 1856. This self-consciousness has been fed by a variety of factors: the discovery of early non-Aryan cultures in India: and the rediscovery of classical Tamil poetry of considerable literary merit.....(Ibid: 2). By claiming a sense of Tamilness for Murugan, the followers of this cult has, no doubt, found meaning for their own Tamilness and Tamil heritage, the sovereignty of which has to be justified to authenticate Tamil's claim for separate self-hood. Thus, Murugan became the medium for articulating both classical and modern ideas (Ibid:2). The terrain of Murugan's body came to relay a whole set of symbols and metaphors. So in true Durkhemien fashion, by worshipping Lord Murugan, Tamils worshipped their own society. In their attempt for reclamation of Murugan along with his Tamilness, leaders of revivalist movements sought to construct a particular way of conceiving Murugan and tried a particular reading of his biography so as to make the image of Murugan the repository of the essential values of Tamil Society. Whereas Clothey identifies a highly unproblematic mirror-like nature of Murugan's image reflecting the changing nature of Tamils self-consciousness, we want to argue that by foregrounding the image of Murugan certain section of politically conscious elite endeavored to construct a particular style and form of consciousness among Tamil populace in order that it may become profitable in realizing the political goals of general Tamil community. We may however agree with Clothey that Murugan cult, popularized by Tamil purists, began to show a remarkable tendency for accommodation of Sanskritic strands in the post-independence period in keeping with the political compromises that Tamil community as a whole had to make when its members realized the impossibility of a separate nation for themselves after independence. (Ibid: 4). Yet it cannot be surmised that the cult of Murugan alone played a crucial role in fueling Tamil's imagination for a coherent moral community. Even from the period during which the quest for independent Dravidian nationhood was intense continuing to the present era, Murugan cult represented only one avenue for arriving at a set of cognitive categories that would encompass Tamil self-consciousness. The flurry of political activities initiated by non-Brahmin movements were constantly cut across by few significant cultural and religious groups, whose idea of Tamilness differed in minor but important respects from that of former. One such group is Saiva Siddhandha Sabha, which had the three-fold purpose of cultivating Dravidian languages, and history, influencing the holders of the religious endowments to eliminate corruption and popularizing what was called the Dravidian religion of 'SaivaSiddhandha (Irschick 1969: 292)

While the cult of Murugan became one of the many cultural media through which Tamil identity was articulated, for those non-Brahmin members who sought to realize their Tamilness in the secular spheres, the imagers of Tamil heroes of the Tamil cinema presented a better option. The anti-religious posture of non-Brahmin movement spearheaded by Periyar meant that it would not side with religious groups like Saiva Siddhandha Sabha, nor with their manner of articulating Tamil identity. Instead of divine images of cults, they chose dramas, novels, open letters and cinema for demonstrating Tamil identity. However, both sections, pro-and anti-religionists, used the persona of God and heroes to arrive at definition of ideal Tamilness.

Fred Clothey rightly anticipates the emergence of secular cults of crypto-religious phenomena having religious connotations and functions, when new-found aspirations outgrow the persona of Murugan (Clothey 19789: 202). Indeed, film personalities are veritable Gods in the secular sphere in Tamil Nadu. Oddly enough even the ardent followers of Murugan cult used the medium of cinema to popularize the cult.

**The Subsumpiton of Symbols of Tamilness in Murugan**

We have already mentioned about the process of classicalisation that resulted in the recovery of ancient literary texts, thereby making them the source book for deriving designs for politics of contemporary Tamil society. It is through this process, the matching of the cognitive categories constructed with the help of classical literature with actual reality was achieved. The essence of all desirable modes was expressed in the form of symbols and metaphors about which mention has already been made above. One of the long-standing images through which these symbols and metaphors sought expression was the image of Lord Murugan. The search for an independent past and recovery of a lost sovereign history attained its summation in the image of Murugan.

Primarily the presentation of Murugan as the archetypal Tamil God is supported by the argument that Murugan is the protector of Tamil language throughout Tamil's history. He is even supposed to have written the preface for Kruntokai (an anthology of Tamil poems dealing with war), and also to have presided over a session in the earlier Sangam (academy of Tamil poets) (Ibid: 24). This apart his service for Tamil is highlighted through narration of incidents: One in which has is believed to have helped Avvaiyar (a poetess who lived during the Sangam period) to recognize the sweetness of Tamil language (Ibid: 86). What becomes relevant to our purpose here is the symbolization of Tamil as Tamilthai (Mother of Tamil) and Murugan as her choicest son, who takes upon himself the task of protecting the purity of Tamil language and implicitly the chastity of his mother tongue, Tamil. This is found in the Bhakthi tradition of Tamil culture, which surfaced during the seventh century (Ibid: 74). It narrates the story of Gnana Sambandha who is believed to be an avatar of Murugan himself. When abandoned by his parents, for Gnanasambandan was born dumb, the goddess of Tamil fed him milk from her breast and then he broke into singing poems in her praise. (Ibid: 87-88). Since Murugan is the child of Tamil Thai many bhakti poets sang in glory of Murugan by visualizing him as a child and themselves as foster parents to whom Tamilthai handed over her own son for nurturance. These poems are available in the anthology, Pillai Tamil (literally, Tamil of childhood) which belongs to the 17$^{th}$ century. Dividing Murugan's childhood into ten stages, these poets affirm their pledge to strive for the protection and purity of Murugan, the son of Tamilthai. Each poet or devotee is exhorted to be his parent as if somewhat responsible for his protection, growth and the extolling of his virtues (Ibid: 57). While in one set of poems preceding the bhakthi period, Murugan himself is the preserver of purity of Tamil, his mother, by foiling the onslaught of asuras (outsiders), in 'Pillaitamil', he himself becomes the protected in the hands of devotees. Murugan's love and respect for Tamil and his adventurous battles against outsiders on the one hand, and the devotees' duty to guard the child so that he can grow and fight against the evil influences on Tamil culture on the other hand express the interlocking of chastity (Karppu) with mother-hood. In a similar fashion Tamilaham (Tamil homeland) gets embodied in Murugan. The Tamil community's attempt to envision and historically ratify a separate territory finds its expression in the way Murugan as the Tamil God resides in different location within Tamil Nadu. Here again one notices the desires to render the cognitive map coterminous with the actual geography of Tamil Nadu. Not only does he personify the antiquity and endurance of Tamil society, but also its hills, fertile landscapes, its origin and its density. The six holy places at which he is believed to have performed some noble feat and to be especially present today are located at very strategic places suggesting the historicity of Tamilaham as these six places cover the territory starting from Thiruchendur in the extreme south to Thiruttani in the north on the one hand and Maruthamalai in the West to Palani in the east (Ibid: 116-128).

Tamilaham as a conceptual category symbolizing the cognitive geography is very important, for this constitutes the outer circle of the concentric circles encircling the other two symbols viz., Centamil and Lord Murugan. The symbol of Tamilaham evokes the imagery of the internal psychic/emotional unity of the members of a household, and by doing so conveys the meaning of the internal psychic/emotional unity of all Tamils. This is Tamilaham about which Pandian has this to say, "Tamilaham is a combination of two words, Tamil and aham (home or interior), which together mean the home of Tamil language, culture and/or people. The symbol serves as a vehicle to comprehend and conceptualize the territorial and cultural boundary of Tamilaham (Tamil Nadu or Tamil country) by contrasting the internal Tamil with the external other". (Pandian.J. 1987: 55).

While all these three symbols recur (either is unison or as combination of any two) when Tamilness is conceptualized, there are some crucial metaphors through which the connections among these symbols are made. We have mentioned the pages above 1. Thai Kulam (Mother community) 2. Kadamai (Responsibility) 3. Irattam (Blood) and 4. Karppu. Discussion of any one these three metaphors,[1] instantly touches upon the three symbols by implication.

Irattam is arguably the most powerful metaphor, finding its place even in the quotidian speech and transactions of Tamils. This becomes the organizing principle not only at the kinship level which has local reach, but also at larger cultural level where it becomes the binding thread linking the entire Tamil community into one coherent whole. Nothing conveys this more succinctly than the following words. In Tamil society "purity is situated in a person's blood (Irattam); blood here does not simply express a biological quality, for it is a term with multiple connotations in Tamil. The movement of blood in the body and its transformation to other body substances is the basis of much south Indian indigenous medicine and is a rich metaphor in daily speech. The form of transmission of this pure blood from parent to child underlies the entire ideology of south Indian caste society.

South Indians say condensed blood can become semen, a repository of purity and power, given its accumulation at the base of the brain through sexual abstinence. In a woman condensed blood can become breast milk. The child is formed from these aspects of condensed blood, as well as from mother's blood directly transferred in the womb. The child then is formed from his parent's blood and inherits the purity that is contained in that blood". (Ostor et.al 1979:13).

At a very immediate level it is through preservation of blood whereby purity of caste is maintained, thus marriage within relatives. But at a wider level, the uniqueness and chastity (Karppu) of the entire Tamil community is guarded, as 'Tamilthai' had fed Tamils whose breast milk is nothing but condensed blood. Hence, it becomes incumbent on every Tamil to strive for the maintenance of purity and chastity of Tamil language and in turn Tamil culture as a whole. The irattam metaphor was effectively utilized by the DMK political leaders whose filiatory politics complemented well with the preexisting belief that Tamil community is an extended clan.

Closely tied with the metaphor of irattam is kadamai (responsibility). This metaphor assumes equal, if not more, importance in the context of the rationalist discourse adopted by the Dravidian Movements (both Dravidar Kazhagam DK and DMK). It is here the past meets the future or, to put differently the traces of modern ideals like equality, rationality, secular sprit, humanism and cosmopolitanism are merged with the essential ancient ideals. Along with other responsibilities of Tamil sons, including that of the preservation of the purity of Tamil language and the chain of identifications that it sets on, the establishment of an egalitarian society in which democracy, humanism and rational beliefs thrive became part of Tamil Kadamai. That DMK in its letterhead, party banners and wall posters included Kadamai as one of the three foremost principles that every Dravidian Tamil was supposed to uphold, only underscores its importance. The primary context in which this metaphor found its dramatic and radical expression was the anti-Hindi movement and the agitation that accompanied it during mid-sixties. In those days the leaders and ideologues of all the Dravidian movements, political parties and literary societies deemed it to be every Tamil's Kadamai to take part in this agitation as it meant the protection of Tamil culture, Tamilthai and Tamil dignity. Describing how this movement brought together both revivalists and rationalists, Sumathi Ramaswami points out the way Tamil language was conflated with Tamil culture and Tamil moral community. She writes "in all their writings and speeches, the Tamil community, metonymically represented by Tamil language and personified by Tamilthai, is a sacralised realm of true and pure Tamil values which all loyal Tamilians were obligated to guard with their lives" (Ramasamy 1993: 704). In the same manner Tamil community was visualized "as distinctive, autonomous racial and political ethnicity (Inam), the sacral center of which is occupied solely by Tamil language, from which all member's claim shared-descent" (Ibid: 704). Besides invoking the symbol of Thai Kulam (Mother community) to motivate the followers to preserve Tamil culture and language, these groups also blended modern ideals. Sumathi Ramasamy's following words capture this: "More striking, in the context of construction and popularization of Dravidian consciousness, rhetorically rooted in claims of rationalist materialism and an iconoclastic irreverence for established religions, is the tremendous secularization in the imaging of language. Great pains (were) thus taken to distance Tamilthai, from any kind of overt religious affiliation, especially those connected with sectarian Shaivite world in which she had first emerged" (Ibid: 706).

What is attempted through these symbols and metaphors, elaborated above, is a construction of Tamil "person" with a unique form of consciousness and style of living. His responsibilities and duties are clearly spelt out; his personhood therefore, becomes rooted in his language, his responsibilities, his homeland etc. It is small wonder that Sumathy Ramasamy concludes this way "Given this understanding of Tamil language, the true Tamil is a thoroughly blended composite of bodily substances, that it would be impossible to severe the language (and the whole chain of significations it suggests) from the Tamil Person". (Ibid : 707).

One can, thus, see a clear linkage between one symbol and another and one metaphor and another. A discussion on any one of them automatically leads to others symbols and metaphors; thereby suggesting some sort of boundedness in the Tamil personhood.

**Symbols in Secular Contexts: A Case Study of a Tamil Film: Manohara**

The previous section dealt elaborately with the way the persona of Murugan became the point at which all symbolic meanings converged to enable Tamils to recoup a history distinctive from a 'sanskritic' 'Aryan' one. By foregrounding the image of Murugan and investing it with historical, social and moral energies, Tamils could achieve some sort of unity of thinking and consciousness, thereby giving a concrete form of Tamil identity. Here, one may clearly discern the intertwining of religious images with secular goals. Despite the anti-religious stance which DMK professed, it acknowledged the significance of the religious imageries in realizing a political end. What is more, it even cashed in on the Tamil chauvinism fueled by Tamil revivalist movements. Yet in keeping with its rationalist and atheistic posture, DK (The parent party whence the DMK, offshooted) led by Periyar E.V.Ramasamy placed less emphasis on the past and made itself more future-oriented (Pandian :1991). This meant certain obfuscation of Tamils' past-centered memory. Thus, while Tamils could reap economic benefits under the tutelage of the D.K, its anti-religious rhetoric and prospectively-realizable nationhood and selfhood fell out of the favour of Tamil populace during 1940's-1950's. To be sure the waning of popularity of the D.K. had a lot to do with other events like Periyar's marriage to Maniammai (a party worker much younger than him) and C.N.Annadurai's decision to break away from the D.K. to form the DMK in 1949. But these events only further accelerated the downward slide, which the D.K. style politics was experiencing. The emergence of the DMK as a major politico-cultural movement marked the arrival of the politics of grand compromise. Its political style was an admixture of its predecessor's rationalism, Tamil revivalism of earlier cultural movements sans their religious disposition, and considerations of electoral politics. Realizing that highlighting of Tamils great past is as important as achieving a dignified future, the DMK envisaged Tamil selfhood, which is also anchored well in the past. For this purpose, it made full use of the achievements of the Tamil revivalist movements – the symbols, and ideals which were made popular by the latter. Frequent comparisons were made between the grandeur of past with the utter decline of Tamils' present. It is around this time that the DMK leaders used Tamil films for political communication. Many of them entered filmdom as actors, script and dialogue writers and film directors. The image of a 'New Tamil person', who is as much an embodiment of virtues of Tamil past as modern ideals like liberalism, rationalism and humanism came to float on the cultural air of Tamil Nadu. Religious imageries like Murugan were replaced, at least by a major section of the DMK leaders, by other renowned figures of ancient Tamil society like Kannagi, Pandian, (the Pandiya King) Karikalan (the Chola king) and of course their clones in modern garbs, in the social films of their period. It is these images, which became the loci around which all symbolic meanings were clustered.

Thus, through a sustained dramatization of these symbols, which had previously existed only in texts and scriptures, the Dravidian movements particularly the DMK, managed to enforce those ideals, which became the defining principles of Tamils worldview and everyday interaction. The ideology of motherhood, love, valour etc. acquired such can encyclopedic character that the contemporary Tamils self-conceptualization practices are drawn from them. One of the powerful media through which the process of dramatization occurred is cinema. Many studies have been done on the role of Tamil cinema in politics, but Tamil films as constituter of a particular style of form of consciousness and Tamils' self-image remains as yet unexplored. This study aims to fill this lacuna.

**Tamilness and Tamil films**

In this section one of the early Dravidian films[2] is analyzed in detail to throw light on the complex thematic and other cinematic practices by which Tamilness was articulated and symbolized. For the purpose of explication, we will consider an important Dravidian film, which was very popular and controversial in its period. It is 'Manohara' (1950). Not only are these Dravidian films crucial from the point of view of their political overtones, but also for their narration of Tamils plight during that period, and their presentation of Tamilness. Nevertheless, these Dravidian films must be distinguished from their predecessors, which we call, "revivalist films". These revivalist films too spoke eloquently of the glory of Tamils and waxed lyrical over their past (Baskaran 1997). These films were inspired by cultural movements[3] aiming to sensitize Tamils to the riches of Tamil culture without any overt political purpose. Interestingly these revivalist films show a lack of a political maneuvouer ability which the Dravidian films had shown. The former set of films restaged Tamil epics like

"Silappathikaram" (1942); Manimekalai (1940) etc., but did not use for the purpose of real politic. In the case of the Dravidian films there was an open invitation to share the concerns and apprehensions of the Dravidian political leaders and ideologues, over the status of Tamil culture and society which were allegedly under the hegemony of North India and its representatives, the Brahmins in Tamil Nadu. Although the cut-off point here is the independence of India and the subsequent arrival of electoral politics, the process by which the Dravidian political party (DMK was founded in 1949) ensured that a constituency among Tamils was well underway even before electoral politics came into effect in 1952 (the first election was held in 1952 and DMK contested in the election only in 1956)

A clear case in point is the film 'Velaikari' (Servant Maid, 1949), scripted by C.N.Annadurai the future chief minister of Tamil Nadu. What united, however, both types of film was the untrammeled eulogization of Tamil culture and Tamil language, in a highly hyperbolic manner. Most of these films were dedicated to Mother Tamil with open sequences showing the image of 'Mother Tamil' followed by a song praising her and Tamil Nadu.

The main theme of many of these Dravidian films was combined with the political message, which was couched in the following formula: The current ruin and degeneration of Tamil Nadu caused by the Aryans, which is a generic term referring to Brahmins, Marvaris and Hindi speakers, can be set right only by a self-respecting rationalist Tamil person. The fractured and humiliated Tamilaham will regain its glory and pride when Tamils rise against the Aryand domination under the able guidance of hero, who is nothing but the Dravidian movement personified. Here again, all the traditional symbols and metaphors were used to good effect to articulate the political message.

Let us illustrate this point by analyzing 'Manohara', a period film set in pre-British era, yet having contemporary political implication. The screen play dialogues for this film were written by Karunanidhi, the scion of the Dravidian movement, who is known for his alliterative and rhymical Tamil usage. It is the story of a king lured by a court a dancer who plots to take over the country by alienating him from his wife and son who is the crown prince. The real queen and prince ultimately succeed in triumphing over the temptress and her cohorts and the latter are put in jail. The film opens with a sequence portraying an intimate domestic scene with the king, queen and the crown prince (Manohara is the character name). This harmony is broken with the arrival of the court dancer. She manages to seduce the king and persuades him to humiliate and ignore the queen and Manohara. In one scene, at the behest of the seductress, he even calls his wife 'whore', the ultimate form of abuse. The son born of the union between the king and the court danseuse is dull-witted, cowardly person whom the temptress wants to be made the future king. There is an interesting characterization here. The son of the temptress, whose attire and few verbal references about her country of origin establish her as an outsider and obliquely, north Indian, is a buffoon and lacks the prerequisites for being a true Tamil person viz, valorous, chivalrous and mother-revering Tamil, whereas Manohara is characterized as one who possesses all essential qualities meant for a 'true' Tamil person. This is established through several dramatic sequences. In a similar vein Manohara's mother is qualified as a true Tamil woman - one who worships her husband even when he abuses her and appears to detest her, one who is patient and enduring great suffering and whose power of chastity can wreak havoc on the enemies- in contradistinction to the 'outsider' woman who is greedy disloyal to her husband and one who is incomplete because of which she begets an incomplete son. Throughout the film, the shots which show the temptress employ 'establishment shots'[4] by which her perennially conspiring nature is affirmed. Whenever, she appears on the screen she appears as a seducer and very few shots show her in isolation from her environment. While dim and low-key lighting characterizes the plight and tribulations of Manoharan's mother, bright lighting and luxurious backdrop qualify the temptress. In contrast to the 'archetypalisation' of Manohara's mother by showing her in isolation with a depthless background and direct address, the temptress always appears to throw her glance laterally as if her filmic existence is derivative of others whom she addresses within the films space and of the lavish objects that surround her.

Coming back to the plot of the film: the seductress hatches a conspiracy with her loyalists against the king to usurp his kingdom form him and put everybody in jail. In the final scene after many dramatic events, Manoharan is chained to a huge pillar by his enemies at which point his mother loses her stoic patience and long-held silence and commands the chains be broken, taking an oath on the chastity. In the following dramatic sequences chains break and Manohara gets the order from his mother to overcome the villains—all of whom are jailed in the climax. The king realizes his folly and return reformed. The family is united. Every one including the general populace, which backed Manoharan to the hilt, is overjoyed.

The role of Manoharan is played by Shivaji Ganesan (a non-Brahmin actor who was a one-time DMK activist) who is celebrated for his versatility and impeccable dialogue delivery. His political affiliation and caste background are very crucial for analysis. Let us take-up an analysis of filmic conventions that were employed to achieve certain symbolic significance for the image. I have already referred to the way in which distinction between good Tamil mother and bad outsider woman is articulated through characterization and shot construction. Here I will look into the signifying practices by which Manoharan's image is figured forth and the kind of ruptures and transgressions that result therefrom.

Whenever, Manohara delivers lengthy dialogues lamenting the present condition of his country, which is in the clutches of outsiders -- the temptress and her cohorts -- he addresses the audience directly, thereby breaking the theatricality, to communicate directly with the audience. The pictorial convention used here is reminiscent of 'iconic aspect'[5]. Here "iconicity of the image" is taken to mean an image onto which symbolic meaning converge and in which moreover, they achieve its stasis" (Kapur 1993:23). Trawick also seems to argue along the same line in her analysis of Paraiyar crying songs. She calls it partial 'isomorphism's or similarities which obtain "between formal properties of a given discourse and properties of the topic of that discourse". (Trawick 1992: 262ff). She goes on to characterize the dissolution of the boundary between the reciting of poem (here it means crying songs) and the real life-circumstances of the recites and audience as "poetic iconicity" (Ibid: 262ff).

Thus, the direct address not only has the symbolic efficacy of elevating (or demoting?) the voyeuristic spectator to non-voyeuristic and active participant in the discourse, but also socializes the spectator into conceptualizing their life-situation in a similar manner. Here this may imply that the audiences are lulled into believing in the present state of ruin, which has befallen Tamil society because of Aryan rule. These signifying practices by which 'iconicity' ("visual iconicity" in line with "poetic iconicity") is achieved is further augmented when the image Manohran is 'frontalised' against a bottomless depth, thereby capturing the image in its pure two-dimensionality and frozenness in space and time (Kapur 1993: 23). This contributes to the 'archetypalisation of the image, foregrounding it as the ideal model available. "The image by virtue of its being positioned and frozen for the non-voyeuristic gaze of the spectators sheds all its quotidian folly to achieve a transcendent and majestic repose: the image here is a type or archetype" (Ibid: 23). This argument juxtaposed to Trawick's, produces a tantalizing image, at once transcendental and phenomenological. This moreover prises open the body of the image in order to allow for the convergence of symbolic meanings[6]. This is further assisted by a deterritorialised and despatialised language, a style of Tamil which is the very opposite of the naïve everyday Tamil used all over Tamil Nadu. Writing on the nature of the spoken word in Tamil films Baskaran states "the language spoken by characters in Tamil films can be described as written Tamil which is different from spoken Tamil (while the former is high the latter is low). The highbrow tamil used on certain occasion is grammatically more complex. It is this form, which is codified and legitimized. This is the written version, which can be used, in a few spoken contexts also such as oration. It is interesting to see that the language in Tamil films too belong to this formal domain. Most of the characters speak the formal or written form. Dialogue in Tamil films is intended to be one-way communication as in a speech from podium" (Baskaran 1997).

While pure Tamil (Centhamil) transcendentalised the image, the place of Centhamil, metonymical of Tamilness, simultaneously brings the image to its phenomenological terrain breaking down the "aesthetic contract" between the text and the viewer. This results in the extension of the textual meaning onto context of viewing. Thus, it upsets the narrative's autonomy and its "radical ignorance of the spectator" to set loose a process of cross signification. Thus, the country for which Manoharan fights becomes Tamil Nadu, his mother becomes the 'Tamil thai' and the humiliation she suffers in the hands of outsiders is taken as attack on mother Tamil. (cf Kapur 1993:19-46).

We have contrasted revivalist films with the Dravidian (or Dravidian-inspired films) in terms of their expressive political orientations. By presenting the glory and greatness of ancient Tamil society, revival films called forth an element of reflexivity from the viewers to compare the days of yore with the present ones. On the contrary the pedagogical objective of the Dravidian films is very overt and visible even in their textural organization of temporalities and spatialities. It is to this aspect we now turn.

Let us try to appreciate the didactic character of these films through an analysis of the way visual devices like point-of-view structure, shot/reverse-shot structure and direct address modes are put to use in the film 'Manohara'. The centrality of point-of-view shots in achieving both pedagogical phenomenological effect has been highlighted by Edward Branigan (1985) and Ravi Vasudevan (1991: 171-85). Point-of-view shots have the potential of constructing the subjectivity of the spectator, through their mode of address and refraction of glances. "Point-of-view is usually understood as the optical perspective of a character whose gaze or look dominates a sequence or in its broader meaning the overall perspective of the narrator towards characters and events of the fictional world" (Stam, et.al 1992: 83).

In the case of 'Manohara' the narrativisation of the events unfolds in a truly Metzian fashion as that which "lets itself be seen without presenting itself to be seen" (Metz 1975:64); as something which happens "in a definitely inaccessible 'elsewhere" (Ibid: 64). However, this is more apparent than true. The theatricality is constantly disrupted and ruptured when the images on the screen abruptly begin to address the spectator directly (about which we have spoken a little above) or when the relaying of glances fails to meet the basic requirement in the point-of-view structure, twice-relayed glances. (For an excellent analysis of the incomplete nature of point-of-view shot and its psychosocial implications (see, Vasudevan 1991: 171-85).

Both forms of rapturing the theatrical contribute not only toward formation of subjectivity but also constituting a political and moral community. Let us look into the ways in which both structures shots, direct-address and frontality on the one hand and non-twice-relayed point-of-view of shot on the other-break down the theatricality and transmute the images into images of pure spectacle. That spectacularisation of images has certain sociological implications warrants such analysis. For example, in a sequence involving Manoharan and his mother, both of whom are conversing with each other over the issue of countering the evil designs of the temptress, one may notice the absence of conventional codes or partial employment of code, to be precise, that would present the event as theatrical. Manoharan expresses his displeasure and anguish over the way his country has been enslaved by the outsiders (temptress and others) and also over the humiliation, which his mother has been subject to, by them.

Here, instead of a conventional reverse-shot structure which implies an alternation of images between seeing and seen and/or point-of-view structure, which anchors the image in the vision and perspective of one or another character, we see direct address being used when 'Manoharan' addresses his mother. On the other hand, when his mother responds to

Manoharan her look is lateral and directed to an off-screen space occupied, here in this case, by Manoharan. Both are highly significant for our purpose. Under normal circumstances the total employment of reverse shot structure and point-of-view shots help the spectators to identify, in effect, with someone who is always off-screen of absent 'other' whose main function is to signify the space to be occupied and equally enable the spectator to become a sort of invisible mediator between an interplay of looks, a fictive participant in fantasy of the film binding the viewers' subjectivity to the text. But the direct address and absolute frontality radically effaces the spectatorial solitude which cinema in the Metzian realist sense invests in the spectator. The atomization of spectators into discrete individuals, forgetful and ignorant of the presence of others in the darkened hall ceases to happen when direct look and subtle exhortations of the image "produce alertness of the subjects to the existence of all others or the alertness of one single subject to the existence of all subjects." (Prasad 1993: 82). It is, in the context of 'Manohara', an invitation to participate in the communal suffering, some sort of a reminder of one's location in the moral community[7].

Another important component of psycho-social modality of spectatorship which point-of-view structure activates is the privileging of the spectator by endowing him/her with the knowledge of the events which the characters in the films are unaware of. Another variant of this case is situation in which the viewers are privy to the knowledge of one single character while all significant others in the film are deprived of the knowledge. We may see the parallel to this situation in 'Manohara' where the audiences are informed of the original wicked nature of the seductress and her conspiracy sessions against the king and his family, through the point-of-view of an amorphous, ghost like character (who is actually the former husband of the temptress who after his premature death, caused by the dancer, follows her to take revenge of her). It is through this 'ghost' that Manoharan too happens to know their sinister plan. The helplessness which both ghost (because it cannot directly intervene into the earthly affairs) and viewers (who cannot intercept the textual flow of events) suffer mobilizes wholesale support and identification with Manoharan whose closeness to the community of viewers is established through his frequent direct address and his mother's relayed look towards him on to an off-screen space filled in by Manoharan[8].

Thus, direct address of Manoharan and lateral look of the mother character although produce rupture and closeness respectively, actually invite the spectator into story-world which progressively fused with the real-world. Paradoxically Manoharan's image becomes the veritable connecting link between two knowledgeable but powerless universes occupied respectively by the ghost and spectators. Interestingly the tension which mounts in us due to our utter helplessness, propels us to place all our faith and hope on Manoharan, the sole saviour.

This is a crucial moment, because it is here the fiction flows into factual world; there is a conflation between narrative time and real time; and the character-narrator ceases to be fictional figure but a real world personality; an indexical figure standing for himself, the actor, and not the character (the iconic figure). By frequent employment of direct address and animating an array of cross-domain referencing practices, the actor playing Manoharan (Shivaji Ganesan) merely extents his role as a DMK activist, emphasising what he actually is in real life. The concerns of Manoharan are real life concerns of Shivaji Ganesan. The audience's urge to resolve the crisis through the agency of Manoharan tends to point up the earning of fundamental complicity of viewers with DMK's mode of articulating and resolving a problem, more importantly with its political vision.

---

**End Notes**

[1] Metaphor is understood here as the derivation of a meaning between things brought together by principle of their similarities.

[3] Here one may recall "Thani Tamil Movement" (Pure Tamil promotion Movement); "Saviva Siddhantha Sabha a part from self-respect movement and south Indian Association, which later merged with Justice party to form Dravidar Khazaham (D.K)

[4] Establishment shots are meant to give an overview of the pro-filmic material so that the close-up of one of one of those material or character makes sense to the audience and guides him to an understanding of where and between whom the dialogue and the action happened.

[5] The inspiration for applying his concept to these filmic practices comes from P.Ricouer, who suggests as to how an image is open to produce surplus significance (See Valdez's 1991: 130-134)

[6] Even now many Rajinikanth's films employ this technique when he conveys a message laden with political significance. In his case not only does the image attain 'stasis' but also a complete transgressive effect (a

kinesics) when the image begins to interact with the audience – a sort of parasocial interaction. The image looks out of the screen and asks questions to the audience in anticipation of fan to answer for them, (which never fails to happen) and jumps into the next question and so on and so forth.

[7] Metz, notes that it is the lack or absence of reciprocal relationship between the actors and spectators that qualifies cinema as a pure theatrical. Unlike theatre where spectators' voyeurism is matched by the actor's exhibitionism that affirms the complicity of both actors and spectators in the whole spectacle, here in cinema the actors are moiré radically ignorant of their spectators. This produces spectator's solitude and enforces direction of energy toward the screen making the film audience more fragmented and isolated, whereas in "theatre, the complicity of actors entails a temporal collectivity among the spectator (Metz 1975:64)

[8] The uniqueness of glance exchanging in establishing 'proxemics' (closeness) with spectators has to be understood here when a character (Manoharan's mother) looks at another (Manoharan) who is momentarily out of frame of else is liked at by him, what is effected here is a primary identification by which everything out of the frame brings us closer to the spectator, that is., one who looks at the frame from outside of it (here Manoharan). It is because the spectator outside the frame and real spectators have point in common: both are looking at the screen (Metz 1975: 57)

CHAPTER THREE

# THE ARRIVAL OF POST-LIBERLISATION TAMIL PERSON

In this chapter we attempt to trace the continuities and ruptures in the way the persona of the Tamil film hero has been structured in the Tamil films. Given the fact that Tamil films have reflected the recent changes in the politics and culture of Tamil society, such a study must assume a historical perspective. Earlier studies tended to focus on the personality of the hero by concentrating more on film scripts and themes rather than on medium-specific features and techniques of film. This critique is based on our firm conviction that more than the image of individual personalities of the Tamil film heroes, it is the supervening nature of the image of Tamil person, which needs to be abstracted out of the countless Tamil heroes, along with the vicissitudes inherent in the thus abstracted Tamil personhood. The symbolic significance of many of the celluloid icons cannot be appreciated independent of the medium-related conventions and techniques. Alongside this, the transformative potency that film as an art form offers in changing a thing or event into a paradigm or a cultural code capable of generating meaningfulness and communicative felicity in the lives of viewers has to be recognized when films or film-related details form the primary data of any research endeavour. (see Andrew 1993:121). In my view this is what is lacking in most studies on Tamil films.

Let us try to evolve an approach, which steers clear of the pitfalls mentioned above. When a study of films of different historical periods is undertaken to capture those moments of discontinuities and transmutations in the history of Tamil man, it is profitable to focus on the structure of the hero's persona in specific relation to other characters and the spatio-temporal dimensions/perspectives within and beyond the filmic text. The processes by which the structuring of the image of hero is accomplished must be brought out. I regard these strategies profitable because in the context of the issues discussed in the previous chapter the actual activation of those symbols and metaphors receives their optimal salience in the interpersonal context of the hero - that is the manner in which he orients himself to other characters, his gestures, his stylistics, his costumes and his actions. If the acquisition of personhood in the Tamil society rests upon one's position in the entire network of relationship, then the same holds true for the image of hero in the film too. Thus, it is by analyzing the structure of inter-personal context in which the personhood of hero receives its fullness, we aim to get close to the codes, which characterize the aspiration- structure of the Tamil middle castes in Tamil society.

It is generally the case that art forms, like novels films, paintings etc. do not herald abruptly alien codes, whose affinity with previous images and themes on the one hand and with socio-cultural experiences of the given society's members on the other, is to be established all anew. They fail to make sense to a given set of individuals because, as Barthes would call it, they have to qualify themselves primarily as anthropological facts, which require some kind of cultural/social apprenticeship before they begin to institute certain forms of meaningful consciousness in the social actors (Barthes 1985:59-60). Hence, the structure of the images of the hero through which historical vicissitudes can be approached may be a carryover from a previous era but lends itself for radical obversion of its previous meanings in new contexts. It is precisely for this reason that we take them as credible data for understanding the social structure of Tamil society. Through a careful analysis of the transformation and equivalents of the structure of the persona of the hero as it obtains in different era, we may identify both the unifying theme of an age and relation between various culturally dominant themes ideas and metaphors.

By carefully and closely examining the inter-personal context within which the persona of the hero takes a concrete shape, we aspire to arrive at a clear understanding of Tamil personhood as an anthropological concept. The diegetic context which functions as miniaturized socio-political universe of Tamil society may become the locus around which contesting aspiration structures and political imaginaries resolve their conflicts symbolically. While different historical periods show certain remarkable transformation in the way the interpersonal context is visualized, one cannot fail to see the equivalences appearing again, albeit with their changed connotations. It is by perceiving that certain basic structures function as cultural codes that communicate culturally relevant information, that one can begin to construct an archeology of imagination, capable of partially re-presenting the way both artists and audiences experience any art form, including films.

Our concern, however, is not just to construct an archeology of imagination and aspiration, but also to trace the genealogy of the Tamil person, the veritable carrier of such imagination. Not only is the notion of the Tamil person helpful in carrying us nearer to an understanding of the politico-economic transformations of Tamil society and of the ideologically inflected constitutive mechanism of Tamil's perception themselves, (in which the role of metaphors and symbols is central), but also crucial in providing the most credible entry point into the filmic text. It is my firm conviction that the concept of the Tamil person refracted through the body of the Tamil film hero, offers itself as the fulcrum around which the symbolic universe revolves.

We have maintained right through this study that cinematic medium is used for the Dravidian political leaders not only to communicate and socialize the masses along the line of political ideals and goals, but also in working out many of their political dilemmas symbolically. To pursue this thesis to its logical conclusion we need to inform ourselves of certain significant political developments during the Dravidian movement. These significant phases can be thought of as crisis moments. More often than not, the developments in Tamil political arena were organically liked to many other variables, the proper appreciation of which can only happen in the light of some decisive events, which mark the history of the politics of Tamil nationalism. It is to these events we turn our attention.

## SPLIT IN THE D.M.K. AND THE ARRIVAL OF M.G.R

By constructing a particular image of Tamil person and endowing it with far-reaching symbolic significance, the DMK. could not only introduce a unique style of self-visualization for Tamil but also use that image as a site for resolving its political dilemmas and for normalizing the compromises it forced to make. That the DMK. emerged as a powerful and popular political party and became the ruling party later in 1960's only suggests that its political style matched with the changing aspiration of Tamil community. Yet the D.M.K's popularity became short-lived when the breakaway group led by M.G.R. formed its own political party, the All India Anna Dravida Munnetra Khazaham (AIADMK) in 1972. This party's arrival and its catapulation to power in 1977 signified the beginning of populist politics. The sociological significance of AIADMK's assumption to power was that it perforce heralded the emergence of lower classes/castes as dominant political actors. This was only to be expected as DMK's style of functioning and its political culture had become somewhat highbrow: That it still attracts larger number of salaried, educated, middle caste supporters, a majority of students; and that its leaders were renowned literary figures and their political discourse shows clear sign of literary refinement sets the D.M.K. apart as a party of middle castes, if not classes. By contrast the ADMK's rank and file consisted mainly of illiterate labourers and women from lower classes. The ADMK's popular leader M.G.R. in all his films and in real life as well skillfully identified himself with the downtrodden and underprivileged who hail from low castes. These notwithstanding, both the D.M.K. and ADMK identified themselves with ideals cherished by Periyar E.V.Ramasamy and Annadurai, although their interpretation of these ideals differed in minor but significant ways. Both parties used the rhetoric's of Tamil dignity. Tamil honour, and anti-Aryanism. The choice of the phrase anti-Aryanism is anything but casual here. While the D.M.K's anti-Brahmin posture continued yet in a mellowed form, the ADMK summarily dispensed with ant-Brahmnism in place of a vaguely defined anti-Aryanism, which, in effect, means anti-Hindi and anti-north Indian policy.

What concerns us, however, our task here is the way they articulated their changing posture. In this respect the period during which Tamil Nadu was ruled by the D.M.K. and the ADMK till 1990's forms one whole and the latter part up to now forms another whole. Assuming, for our present purpose, that the process of liberalization of the Indian economy initiated by successive governments at the center proved to be a watershed in India history, we term the first pre-liberalisation period and the second the post-liberalisation era.

In the pre-liberalisation era both the DMK. And the ADMK did not show any radical changes in the way they envisaged Tamilness. They, to be sure, constantly negotiated with and redefined the notion of Tamilness, although only within the ambit pre-given classical symbols and codes of which we have spoken at length in the preceding chapter. Their approaches and the differences in them were limited only to matters of detail and not of type. During all these years both parties used Tamil cinema as an effective medium to comment upon each other's policies and functioning. Their political goals which were centred upon strategies that would help them to expand and retain constituency of supporters, were mediated through films. Anyhow both had to return to the fundamental question of who is a Tamil.

When the DMK emerged as a political party, it did so under the shadow of success of its precursor the D.K. which during the pre-independent era professed the policy of pan-Dravidian unity. Subsequently the DMK itself adhered to the policy of secession from Indian Union well into 1950's, demanding a separate nation-state (Dravida Nadu) for all those who speak one or other Dravidian languages. All these meant that the question over the exact nature of Tamil identity was not to be taken seriously until mid-fifties. That both the D.K in its ranks and Madras State, before it was reorganized along language lines in 1956, had consisted of people speaking all four languages which belong to the Dravidian family, easily rendered discussion on the exclusive nature of Tamil identity suspect. However, revivalists operating within the territory of what became later known as Tamil Nadu, engaged themselves with this question in a different way. Once the independence of Indian, the state reorganization along linguistic affiliation, and electoral politics became established, the focus was shifted to Tamil Nadu (then Madras state). Ever since Tamil Nadu became the sole zone of operation for the DMK, the processes leading to crystallization of Tamil identity received further impetus. It is around this time issues such as Tamil blood, Tamil dignity Tamil racial community, Tamil culture, Tamil territory all became absolutely interchangeable terms.

As we have analysed in the previous chapter, these discussion and issues had their reverberation in films of that period. Indeed, it is through films that categories by which Tamil identity was constituted were invested with an aura of factuality. The propriety of an act or a cultural product is thought to be vested in the verified identity of a Tamil person. These questions were raised with utmost vigour by the DMK politicians when the ADMK came to power in 1977. If the DMK initiated a discussion on Tamil identity as having its origin in Tamil blood, through films and other forums, M.G.R. had to reconstruct the notion of Tamil personhood along a different line, in keeping with his outsider status[1]. Thus M.G.R. had to push aside the over-determining nature of Tamil blood as giver of Tamil identity, instituting in its place some other principle, to validate the propriety of his claim for Tamilness. Therefore, M.G.R. throughout the second half of his film-acting career had to wrestle with the problem of outsider status and with legitimization of "achieved Tamilness".

A careful analysis of M.G.R.'s films leads to proper understanding of the changed codes through which he articulated Tamilness. Contrasting the persona of MGR as he presented himself through his films with the celluloid image Shivaji Ganesan -- a versatile actor whose D.M.K. days preceded that of MGR—during the early part of pre-liberalisation period, will aid us to capture, synoptically, the larger social processes that were operative during their respective periods. It is with the help of this comparative perspective we hope to understand the radical shift that Tamil identity has taken in recent days.

## *IDEOLOGY OF BLOOD OR CODE OF CONDUCT*

Given the Dravidian-sponsored understanding of Tamil community as an extended clan wherein all the members are united by a putative singularity of blood, it immediately necessitates an account of kinship context within which identity achievement becomes realizable for a Tamil. Drawing upon Stephen Barnett's (1975) study of Kondai Katti Vellala (KV), a non-Brahmin 'Vegetarian' caste, we wish to throw light on the principles governing the kinship system. Barnett identifies two principles that operate in the kinship system of KV members. They are the principle of natural identity (or inherited biogenetic substance transmitted from parents to children) and code of conduct (guide to correct behaviour)" (Barnett: 150). He further argues "sexual intercourse is the core symbol that links relations through natural identity and conduct and through conduct alone" (Ibid : 150). The importance of these two principles is affirmed when he states, "substance and codes are thought of in terms of blood and the physical body in the south Indian theory of conception and procreation. Blood is the locus of purity, and blood purity is transmitted from both parents (semen is concentrated blood, breast milk is also concentrated blood since the fetus may also absorb uterine blood) to children. If a person does not conform to caste codes for conduct, blood purity is affected and can result in outcasting." (Ibid: 151). Although codes and substance were interlinked in the past, thanks to urbanization, democratization of polity and modernization of society, there seems to have been a delinking of substance from code. "This changes the way blood purity is conceptualized, thus paying the way for new components of personal and social identity.... Ideas of race, ethnicity, cultural nationalism and class become thinkable only, given a separation of substance and code. (Ibid:151). What results at a macro level, if we extrapolate these concepts, is of immense significance. Barnett points to this when he argues "south Indian castes now resemble ethnic groups; untouchables are excluded from ethnicisation and are coming to be thought of as a separate race: Tamil cultural nationalism posits a common code for all castes..." (Ibid: 151). I consider the last few lines very important for our analysis. Just as political processes have led to a separation of code from substance at the local level, ethnic identity of Tamils came to hinge as much upon the code of conduct which has been defined by the Dravidian movement under the rubric of Kadamai (see the previous chapter for and extensive discussion on this theme) as upon one's blood. Yet, blood or substance itself does not remain static; not only does it get altered during one's life time because of violation of codes of conduct, but, as Valentine Daniel has brilliantly argued, it (substance) becomes even achievable through right conduct in a proper socio-geographical context (Daniel 1987: 71). Explicating his case through his study of another Vellala caste, Arnot Vellala (AV), he puts forth the thesis that one's fundamental body substance, which assigns him an identity, gets fundamentally altered and because of transsubstantialisation the person begins to acquire a different substance altogether (Ibid : 74). This boils down to rendering ethnic Tamil identity dependent not only upon one's possession of Tamil blood, but also independently upon code of conduct.

In the light of this we may suggest that the two-way entry available to Tamils is the consequence of the arrival of electoral politics and the wholesale economic rewards attendant upon it. It is in the period that Barnett and Daniel carried out their studies (around mid 70s) that M.G.R. emerges in the cultural horizon of Tamil Nadu seeking Tamilness on his own. In the following pages I attempt an analysis of the way M.G.R negotiated the conception of Tamilness, by contraposing his image to that of Shivaji Ganesan[2].

Once again this brings us face to face with Tamil popular films. While the DMK sought to ascribe to itself the role of the preservation of Tamil culture by articulating its claim through Tamil films, M.G.R. too had to perform the twin-task of assuming the role of guardian of Tamil dignity which he alleged, was in a degenerate position due to the D.M.K's misrule; as well as striving to legitimise his "achieved Tamilness." The fact that moviegoers made constant references to cross-domain realities when endorsing a cultural product or in validating the propriety of some one's claim for Tamilness mean that social actors seeking general political or cultural power/authority had to affirm their Tamilness through their conduct and actions. Thus, the film-viewing environment was surcharged with cross-referencing and multiple interpretive regimes. The audience enters into the reception contexts with background information concerning the product and the actors involved producing it.

Pursuing this argument that the process of authenticating a cultural material like film and according it a sense of Tamilness is necessarily intertextual, we may take up some of the films of Shivaji Ganesan and M.G.R. We have limited ourselves to a discussion of thematics of the concerned forms without making penetrative textual analysis, for our concern here is to provide a backdrop against which the major transformation of the Tamil person can be analysed through a full-fledged textual analysis of recent Tamil films.

## *ASCRIBED TAMILNESS Vs. ACHIEVED TAMILNESS: THE PERSONAE OF SHIVAJI GANESAN & M.G.R*

Shivaji Ganesan offers an interesting social type when placed in the context of our study. He offers himself as an archetypal example of a person whose Tamilness is indubitable. His caste (he comes from a non-Brahmin Maravar community, one of the notable constituents of the compendium of castes whose members make up the ranks and file of both the Dravidian parties) identity complements his ethnic identity when the criterion of substance is applied.

This mirrored very strongly in the films in which he is depicted as having an unbroken and complete kinship network. References are made to the fact that both his parents are alive. This is depicted in various ways, either as a verbal reference or as a photographic assertion or as actual alive presentation. Thus, he derives his familiarity and identity from/in a domestic group in which he is an actual 'insider'. In contrast to M.G.R films which portray his movement from a position outside the domestic context (consider the symbolic meaning of Tamilaham Tamil-home) into an 'adopted insider', Shivaji Ganesan's 'insider' status reaches summation in a complete domestic context. Even the sibling ties which Shivaji Ganesan's character maintains in the films are actual rather than 'won' by demonstration of love. In Parashakthi (1956), Ganesan (Gunasekaran his character name ) is firmly tied to his siblings whom he recovers in the climax. By a significant intermixing of textual and extra-textual references the Tamil personhood of Shivaji Ganesan is strongly established in his films. This is also evident in the way his character is identified with a caste name, though rather obliquely, by reference to character's father or father's-in-law name which would carry the caste tag along with them. Yet the issue of caste identity has been downplayed largely in his political films, in which the main protagonist is portrayed as one whose disdain for superstition religious dogma are the hallmark of the Dravidian person, as it was imagined by the Dravidian movement. When his case is contraposed to that of M.G.R. interesting insights may be gleaned out.

The fact that Tamilness-derivable-from-the-Tamil-blood thesis remained improbable for M.G.R, it rendered his mobility within Tamil cultural landscape highly problematic. To win a license, as it were, for an insider status, M.G.R. had to resort to the second option, that is, adherence to the code of conduct laid out by the Dravidian movement. Tamilness by achievement, as against Tamilness by ascription, presented itself as the only avenue through, which M.G.R. gained an entry into the Tamil social region by his unstinting commitment to uphold the values of Tamil society.

This is evidenced more palpably in his films. In all his films M.G.R. appears as an incomplete person, incomplete because he is either an orphan or he only has his mother, with his father's identity remaining vague and unclarified, because he is a 'social outcaste'[3].

He is introduced in majority of his films as a kinless individual, his ties yet to be established and earned. He normally advances from a position where he does not have kin group of his own into one where he wins the heart and faith of a set of individuals who adopt him into their kinship network as their own son. This complements his outsider status in real life, who presses his claim for Tamil personhood through a demonstration of intense commitment to Tamil values. This meant that in his interpersonal relationship, M.G.R. wins sisters, mothers, brothers and others by his good deeds. This explains why M.G.R. presented himself as a pure type assuming the values of Tamil culture in such an uncompromising manner. His portrayal of his image (M.G.R took his roles very seriously and was very particular about even minor details (Pandian 1992:96) as an immediate Tamil who is chivalrous, respecter of his mother and Tamil Language who is morally upright (though a thief of underworld don), protector of Tamil and Tamil land and one who is never self-indulgent (M.G.R. never smoked or drank alcohol in his films) so on and so forth, clearly confirm his attempt to erases his outsider status. While petty concessions were given to the son-of-soil hero Shivaji Ganesan, who represented himself in many of his films as a spoiled brat who womanized, gambled and drank liquor, the same were not available to M.G.R. as they would have endangered his staking a claim for membership within the moral community of Tamils.

Continuing our interpretation of the interpersonal context within which Shivaji Ganesan and M.G.R's Tamilness was realized, we may dwell upon their modes of orientation to the fellow characters within the filmic representations of these actors. It is true that both actors chose a well-defined kin matrix to obtain their Tamil persona, though their modus operandi differed in significant ways. Besides this, however, their orientation to others in the filmic universe is not dissimilar at all.

In keeping with the principle of filiations that pervades the entire Tamil society, their significant relationships consist only of kin with even the strangers-who-became-friends being converted into kin through marital alliance. In the off-screen lives of these actors and other Dravidian party leaders, the notion of putative unity of all Tamils who are divisible roughly into affinal and consanguineous relatives had its echo in the way friends address each other using kinship terminologies and in the way Dravidian leaders salute their followers using expressions like " "Blood of my blood" and "blood brothers and sisters". This is more evident in the manner heterosexual bondings are represented in Tamil films of the old days as is discussed below.

The political imperative that Tamil society has to be construed as consisting of members who are related to each other, has left no space for stranger within the ambit of Tamil community. However, the strangers may be adopted into the Tamil community if they are ritually deracinated of their original identity and adhere to the code of conduct meant for the Tamil moral community. Thus, Tamil society is characterized essentially by fraternal ties with space allocated for potential mates whose connection to the ego is again blood-determined (Ostor et.al. 1979). This is an important reason why heterosexual friendship has never been discussed as a possibility in Tamil films. Both M.G.R. and Ganesan's numerous films show them treating the women they encounter within the textual space as mothers and sisters, when they are not their wives/lover girls.

In the case of strangers, who are virtual outsiders because they are not ritually accommodated into the social universe of Tamil's by addressing them using kin terms, their non-Tamilness is characterized by their non-inclusion and their potential threat to the unity and integrity of Tamil community. The temptress in the film 'Manohara', with all the attributes suggestive of her non-Tamilness poses such a threat. When the strangers' threat has been muted because of their accompaniment in the mission of hero, they still retain their state as stranger by being susceptible to stereotypicalisation. Here one may consider "national integration "films like 'Bharata Vilas' starring Shivaji Ganesan who resides in a big house along with fellow residents who are from other linguistic groups and religions. Although a sense of camaraderie prevails among them, they are more like friends that relatives. While any fellow Tamil character is likely to be fitted into the kin network, outsiders are stereotyped in to standard roles: Malayali are Nayars, north Indians are always Marwaris and they are even addressed as such.

Commensurate with the imagination that a Tamil speaking non-Brahmin Dravidian populace forms a well-knit moral community, the filmic image of the Tamil hero's social world is presented as miniaturized universe reflecting the world outside the screen, although such a reflection is ideologically inflected.

The interpersonal environments of relationships were inhabited by personae of potential and actual relatives, stereotyped strangers and also by a close-knit kin-unit very immediate to the hero. In the case of Shivaji Ganesan it is mostly pre-given, whereas M.G.R. achieves it at the end. By closely-bound kinship unit, I mean that which comprises siblings, parents, grandparents and occasionally arriving but well-defined relatives - father and mother-in-law and those who are related to them. This aspect of the interpersonal environment is very important when we analyse recent films. Thus, I leave this point here so that it can be picked up later.

To sum up the arguments given above: one needs to place the event of M.G.R's arrival as a significant political and film personality in the context of the changing politico/economic realities in Tamil Nadu. The changed circumstances, particularly the overbearing presence of Indian nation-state as an important entity in influencing the life-chances of Tamils, necessitated a radical change in the terms and categories through which the collective aspiration of Tamil community was articulated. Besides this, Tamils had to continuously negotiate the indisputable fact of outsiders coming into

Tamil Nadu as much as insiders going out of Tamil Nadu in search of better economic opportunities. The emergence of M.G.R was influenced by these social trends.

As a logical next-step one is obliged to consider the case of Rajinikanth here. Once again, the question of outsider lurks starkly behind Rajinikanth's persona. This may be juxtaposed to Rajinikanth's controversial statement made during his interview to a TV network recently. When asked how can he, being an outsider, (he is a Maharashtrian by birth) hope to play a crucial role in Tamil politics, he answered "all those who live in Tamil Nadu and speak Tamil can claim Tamilness (Gnani, 1996). Rajinikanth's political ascendancy too has a long history. He entered Tamil filmdom around 1970's as a villain and within a decade was transformed into a superstar hero.

Rajinikanth's ascending career graph went side by side with the decline of chauvinist Tamil movements. The unbridled nativism, once the trademark of the Dravidian movement, was getting diluted as people were busy expanding, their zone of operation in search of employment and business opportunities across the border of Tamil Nadu. Most important social actors here are the second generation educated non-Brahmin Tamil youths whose training in and exposure to the classical literary tradition of Tamil community and the doctrines of the Dravidian movements are at best second hand and text-bookish, if not negligible. This new generation grew more and more distant from the past struggles which the Dravidian movements had waged. Moreover, the numerous openings which the Dravidian movement created for the non-Brahmin youth - in education particularly – propelled them to hanker for opportunities outside Tamil Nadu. These opportunities in educational institutions and employment sectors outside Tamil Nadu, came in the way of Tamils puritanical predispositions- particularly the pre-existing contempt for Hindi and the culture of north India. The educated youth had to reconcile themselves with the emerging situations, for which new compromises had to be made. Linguistic affinity in its radical version had to be toned down. It is in this context Rajnikanth's advent had to be placed. Here is a personality whose claim for Tamil identity is limited to his speaking the language, only in its everyday colloquialism, not in its pristine form. His adherence to Tamil values again being selective and practical. The era in which the heroes who uttered Tamil poems, couplets and quotations from the classical Tamil texts is gone. For the present-day youth is as ignorant about these literature as about the historical struggles waged by their father generation. In many M.G.R. and Shivaji Ganesan's films not only can one listen to songs in which Tamilthai will be praised, but can also see the heroes holding Thirukkural (an ancient book of aphorisms) or Bharatidasan's poetry books (Bharatidasan was the official poet of the Dravidian Parties).

In many of Rajinikanth's films he enters into the narrative without clarifying his origin. Even the narrative does not bother to explain this aspect, only his name and the language he speaks characterize him as Tamil. A typical case in point is the film "Badshah" (1995). This is a politically very significant film as many of its dialogues were read off as Rajinikanth's responses to Jayalalitha whom Rajinikanth was opposed to in principle during the assembly and parliament election in 1995. Here in this film Rajinikanth (Manickkam is his character name) is an auto driver who lives in a family consisting of his foster mother and her grown-up daughter and son. The family he lives with and the environment in which he moves about are distinctly Tamil, even though Rajinikanth's Tamilness is limited to his speaking his language and carrying a pure Tamil name. At no point in the entire narration is his origin traced completely, barring a couple of occasions when his exploits as a rowdy in a Bombay slum are referred to. His sudden arrival into Tamil Nadu and his involvement in a Tamil family remain unhinged facts.

What is clearly lacking in Rajinikanth's films is a well-defined kinship network. His entry into narrative as a marginal man who gradually moves into the center stage complements suited his outsider status. While he has a foster family, he is seen to operate more in the public territory aided by his occupation as a coolie, auto driver, milk-vendor and so on. This appears to be a departure from the social film genre of the previous period although, it takes off from the political films of the Dravidian movement in terms of their elaboration of public landscape instead of the familial space, which is privatized. In many of M.G.R's films too one can see the foregrounding of public over familial, in contrast to Shivaji Ganesan's films, the streets in M.G.R. and Rajinikanth films are not transitory zones, rather they are the destinations which the hero seeks to reach. Since the familial domain is unavailable to them as they are outsiders in ethnic terms, they strive for Tamilness in the impersonal terrains, which are streets. To achieve this, they select gestures and actions, which are inappropriate in the kinship context. Yet in the end the street is pulled into familial context when the heroes manage to acquire families of their own, mainly through their being adopted by a pre-existing kin-network. It is however, the streets to which they return, but this time as insiders. This is in stark contrast to the American western genre films, wherein the cowboy hero enters and exits from the narrative as an outsider.

As regards the transgressive demeanours of the vagabond cowboy hero, Jameson details the narrative sequences in which the hero's abundant creatively destructive energies are elaborated; how he decimates the marauding raunchers an how he transforms the dry and arid zones into verdant landscapes with his hard work are instances. These actions are contrasted to the impotency and docility of societal members, the typical of them being represented in the form of Cowboy's lover's husband. Yet the plenitude of raw libidinal energy of the Cowboy hero needs to be disavowed, contained and kept within bounds as it possesses potential threat to social order. Aside this, his bodily movements, his gestures, dress codes, actions, language, name, etc. reiterate his violative posture that he strikes towards the social order. They mark him off as a clear outsider who can never integrated into the social order unless his transgressive potency is made null and void.

Seen in this light one may see parallel tendencies operating in the case of Rajinikanth's persona, although the manner in which his threat gets cancelled out has political underpinnings specific to the time and space he belongs. Like the Cowboy hero, he too is ranked as an outsider both in the filmic text and in real life as well. The outsider status renders his acts of transgression quite normal and unsurprising. Cast this way, his violative buffoonery earns the approval of the marginalized and silenced ones whose anger, directed towards the economically advanced middle castes and upper castes in Tamil Nadu, finds expression through the image of Rajinikanth. The psychological and physiognomic affinities between the latter and an average youth from an economically underprivileged middle or lower caste account for Rajinikanth's phenomenal popularity among youths. The caste and class characters of the young male members, who virtually take over the streets and theatres screening Rajinikanth's films in the initial days after the film's release, are that of lower class and low-middle caste.

The emergence of economically impoverished middle caste, lower cast nexus appearing in the shape of a new political party launched by Ramadoss, a low middle-caste physician, in 1980's signal the heightened political awareness among the sections of low middle and low castes. These castes remained largely on the fringes of the Tamil moral community and hardly benefited for, the political achievements of the Dravidian parties. This party P.M.K., Pattali Makkal Katchi (Toiling People's Party) though owing allegiance to the key figures of the Dravidian movement particularly E.V.R.Ramasamy, has expressed its discontent with the D.M.K. and the A.D.M.K. accusing them of siding with the economically rich middle caste. Despite its negligible success, this party has kindled the political consciousness of many low and middle caste youths, who are becoming increasingly critical of the Dravidian politics. They, mainly school dropouts and blue color workers, are staunch admires of Rajinikanth. Their selective adherence to Tamil nationalist ambition, coupled with their marginalized outsider status (outsider from the viewpoint of the Dravidian politics) finds its vicarious identification with Rajinikanth. They regard such identification meaningful and culturally relevant. Their desire to parody and ridicule the behaviour of the rich and educated realizes its tangible expression in Rajinikanth's bodily demeanour which scoffs at and violates rather gleefully the upper-class attitude and mores.

In many of Rajinikanth's films not only does he outsmart foreign-returned and polished competitors in the race to win the love of the heroine, but also moves in the upper class spaces - palatial houses, five-star hotels; sanskritised higher-caste owned temples and music and dance schools -without compromising his surly, unrefined manners associated with the underprivileged youth. The choice of homes, mostly connotative of low-caste origins, his occupation as auto driver, server, servant-boy etc. and his dress codes, which are a bricolage of upper class attire in combination with patently subversive and satiring apparel suggestive of a rural and unsophisticated character all seems to reiterate his disrespect for upper and middle caste/class norms and mores. In many of his films he may be seen wearing a double-breasted rich-looking suit, an upper class insignia, but at once subverted by a cotton towel wrapped around his waist or by his deliberately slovenly posture marked by clumsy gait, egregious color combination (yellow trousers and red shirts) and so onWhat implication do these contravening gestures have for the configuring of the 'aesthetics of the under privileged' in the political and everyday concerns of Tamil society? While the former aspect awaits its tangible manifestation (the real politic is yet to lend an ear to the voice of underprivileged) the latter aspect has its recorded proofs in the way the fan followers of Rajinikanth, hailing from the edges of Tamil society (working class, Dalits - mainly school drop-out youths) who underline their presence rather vociferously when they open 'new Fan clubs' or when they whiz down city streets on their cycles, autorickshaws, and Taxies to watch the films of Rajinikanth just released. On these occasions, they literally take over public spaces, streets and theatre premises (spaces occupied rightfully by elders and educated middle class/ caste public) and convert them into regions of carnival. It is quite common to see them shouting, and howling at general public on their way to cine halls.

It is not surprising the street as a public space acquires such far reaching political significance both in Rajinikanth's films and in the daily lives of his fans. In the case of former it is the street and the interpersonal context that it supplies, from which he moves into the domestic sphere, to return back to the street as an 'insider. But in the latter case it is the same street where his fans announce their arrival in the public discourse.

## *POST-LIBERALISTION FILMS: RECODING THE NOTION OF TAMIL PERSON*

What post-liberalisation films have to say about a Tamil person is more interesting. The scenario is set by Mani Ratnam's 'Roja' (1993) followed by his own 'Bombay' (1994). Also important in this respect are films like 'Kadhal Desam' (1996) and 'Minsara Kanavu' (1997). All these films have been directed by young urbane, cosmopolitan, middle and upper caste movie directors.

Driven by the desire to exploit the expanded market, these posts-liberalization films show a clear departure from the dominant mode in which Tamilness was visualized in old films. The interpersonal context within which the Tamil hero journeys is dotted with English speaking, educated women, working mothers, bevies of girlfriends and friends who are not transformed into sisters and brothers respectively. By and large, the hero's environment smacks of cosmopolitanism and multiculturalism. Unlike the films of the past, in which the kindred formed the backdrop, the recent slew of films foregrounds a nuclear family, the last irreducible unit of consumption in the modern era. Take for example the recently released 'Kadhal Desam (Love Nation) and 'Minsara Kanavu" (Electric Dream). In both these films we have heroes accompanied by his poor friends. While the rich friend and his poor companion in 'Kadhal Desam' do not have a family of their own, the poor friend in 'Minsara Kanavu' has only friends but no family. In both films, poor heroes strike close resemblance to an average Tamil, whereas the rich in both films look exceptional and outlandish. This is anything but casual. Although all characters are Tamils in that they speak Tamil, the cosmopolitan look of Aravind Swamy (in Minsara Kanavu) and Abbas (in Kadhal Desam), might help the pass off as residents of any region within India. No attempt is made to establish the Tamilness of the characters (barring Arvindswamy's case where he is identified as Nadar, a mercantile community which is fast widening its business networks across Tamil Nadu) in any other form whatsoever. Even the locale within which the actors move about is a highly manipulated location, maneuvered to jive with cosmopolitan looks of the heroes (see below for an elaborate discussion).

The nature of friendship between both the pair in both films is surprisingly uncomplicated with both addressing each other as just friends and not using any surrogate name for brothers. The way heterosexual friendship is presented in these films proves to be intriguingly significant as it makes a visible movement away from conventional form of narrativisation. A brief description of the themes of the respective films might be of some help here. In 'Kadhal Desam', it is a story of two-college-going students, who fall in love with the same girl without, predictably, knowing that the other person also is in love with her. Close friends that they are, each is prepared to sacrifice his love for the girl when realization dawns. Not willing to break their intimate friendship, the heroine decides to treat both of them as good friends for life, as choosing one as a marriage partner may break their friendship.

In ' Minsara Kanavu', it is once again a triangular love story. The rich and poor heroes try to woo the same girl, but with a difference. The poor hairdresser friend (Prabu Deva) helps his rich friend (Aravindswamy) by persuading her to change her mind so that she can give up her ambition to become nun and marry the rich man(Aravinda Samy). But in the process of converting, the heroine and poor hero fall in love with each other. The climax arrives with rich man choosing to remain as a friend to the heroine permitting the hairdresser friend to marry her.

These films are significant as they problematize the filial nature of moral community, by positing inter-sex friendship as a possibility. Both these films have been shot in film-city with only few scenes being shot in outdoor locations. The entire castings in these films showcase cosmopolitanism at its best. Roping in actors from far and wide of India (the heroines of these films are from the Hindi Film Industry) these films look capable of qualifying as native stuff wherever they are released after being dubbed in the local language. In their drive to foster a pan-Indian character, even the cultural markers specific to Tamil society have been carefully erased, both in terms of theme selection and pro-filmic details, filling the frames. By successfully deterritorializing these films, the rupture that may arise out of participation in different cultural location has been dispensed with too.

These films mark the arrival of a new post-liberalization era in which films are oriented to the national market for making profit. The arrival of a new generation of Tamils, more urbane than their predecessors, the opening of the national market and its repercussions at local levels, and the communication revolution in India, all have called in to question the validity of existing categories of cultural practices and old form of imagining of Tamil moral community. This is reflected in the image of the hero one may see in the recent set of films in which the heroes are career bureaucrats working for the national government. The implementation of the Mandal Commission recommendations reserving the seats for other Backward Classes (under which majority of non-Brahmin youths could make use of the national level resources and opportunities), suddenly open up the national level opportunities for the other backward castes (OBCs) among whom, the OBCs from Tamil Nadu stand at the frontier. This calls for shedding old fetters like linguistic chauvinism, rigid cultural identifications and so on. One is definitely struck by the frequency with which one encounters movies title “Tamil Selvan I.A.S”, “Vyjayanti I.P.S”, “Sethupathi I.P.S” and so on, denoting a vast change in the attitude of Tamil populace. Similarly, the felicity with which the heroes in “Kadhal Desam” and ‘Bombay’ loiter around the streets and locales of Bombay, Kashmir, and Delhi not as tourists but as residents have broken the existing codes through which the Tamil person had been hitherto visualized. As an illustration let us end this chapter by mentioning a telling sequence which occurs in ‘Roja’ where the conversation between the hero and his mother takes place in English, while the hero smokes cigarette in front of his mother -- something unthinkable in the past in which mother and mother tongue were regarded as objects of reverence and worship.

To sum up this chapter we can sensitize the reader to the changes in the way Tamil personhood has been conceived, against the background of the symbols and metaphors we have elaborated in the last chapter. It is not difficult to notice the dynamisation of certain operational terms and their dilution, across the history of the contemporary Tamil society. The codes which came to characterize the classical conception of Tamil person and the articulation of the same by a panoply of forces, political parties, cultural and religious movements and social reform movements, during the decades immediately antecedent to and following the independence of India, were either broken down because they (codes) proved to be restrictive or they were recoded with new meaning attached to them, because changing political and social situations so demanded. This chapter tried, as it did, to recount the story of Tamil person as he was typified in Tamil films. In the next chapter an attempt is being made to analyze the notion of Tamil selfhood and subjectivity.

---

## *End Notes*

[1] Public wisdom, considered M.G.R. as an outsider because he was Malayali by birth and his birth place itself is in an alien territory, Srilanka.

[2] It must be remembered that the political career of S.Ganesan is marked by multiple affiliation with parties ranging from regionalist to nationalist. He was initially a member of the D.M.K then left it for the congress around the 1960's and his later days he associated himself with Janata Dal and then launched own political party in the late 1980's. We treat both actors as successive to each other in the light of their political affiliation. The space left by Shivaji was taken up by M.G.R.

[3] M.G.R., in most of his films clearly identified himself with low caste members, either by his occupation – as an agricultural labour, or a rickshaw driver or a pickpocket etc.—or by his choice of neighbourhood –he primarily emerged from slums-or by his immediate interpersonal context-his friends are poor slum dwellers (Pandian 1992:39). This, in effect, relegated him to the margins of Tamil culture, because Dalits or (Panjamas as they are called) stood outside the purview of Dravidian Tamil community.

CHAPTER FOUR

# FROM PRODUCER TO CONSUMER: THE BIRTH OF THE TAMIL SUBJECT-IN-CONSUMPTION

If the primary concern of the previous chapter was to trace the genealogy of the Tamil person in juxtaposition to the Tamil's modern political history, the present purpose is to use the very historical knowledge as the backdrop of our analytical description of Tamil subjectivity as it moved from the post-liberalization phase. In the preceding chapter the notion of person was understood and treated as an anthropological concept which accounted for our analysis of the kin and inter-personal context of the respective films, whereas presently we intend to engage ourselves with an exploration of the changing nature of subjectivity which the Tamil films have aimed to institute in the minds of Tamil viewers. This, in our view, needs to be addressed urgently, because the political facet of Tamil selfhood, is being problematised and recast in current situations. The subject-in-struggle generation is fast giving way to subject-in-passive consumption under the transformed political and economic circumstances of the present day.

Thus, one again we proceed to analyze the commercial Tamil films by approaching them through an interpretation of the manner in which two of the most important filmic conventions are deployed. They are point-of-view structure and narrative distance. In some important senses both are interrelated, even though they are analytically separable. They are interrelated in that the former entails the latter. As we have demonstrated in the previous chapter, the incomplete nature of point-of-view shot can result in partial or total abolition of narrative distance between the viewer and the viewed[1]. (R.Vasudevan 1993 and Braingnen 1985).

It is worth pointing out there that point of view and shot/reverse shot structures are not the only devices by which narrative distance can be abolished or established as the case may be. Some other modes, which come immediately to one's mind, are the synchronisation/disjunction in sound-image dichotomy, verbal references to certain real-life occurrences and so on.

It is very important that we take up another related and crucial concept at this juncture: Estrangement. In an important sense both narrative distance and estrangement are inversely related. When narrative distance is reduced to a minimum or eliminated altogether the viewer feels estranged totally from the narrative. This led to a situation in which the viewer's voyeurism is aborted fully. Thus, instead of deriving pleasure from the text into which the viewer is 'sutured', he/she begins to experience estrangement and unpleasure. This is very important for our analysis. To anticipate the arguments put forth in the later part of this chapter, we may mention that these politically important films, through an association by contiguity and by similarity (or metonymically and metaphorically, to borrow Jakobson's terms[2]) remind the audience of the yet-to-be-waged struggles in real life. They do this by drawing the audience into the narrative space and time through deployment of direct address and incomplete point-of-view structure, though not always consciously. These films instead of functioning as predominant means mobilizing desires and producing pleasures, refuse pleasure and point toward the political and moral responsibilities of the viewers. As the image of the hero is decisive here, it is the way hero's image is configured by which audience is commandeered to be in the midst of the thick of political action.

It denies jouissance and induces anguish as it keeps the viewers close to the center of the dusty field of political struggle, calling forth the viewers to morally sympathize with hero's image. His plight is sought to be shared by the audience and not to be enjoyed from an intellectual and moral vantage-point somewhere outside the text/event. To put it crudely, by depriving the viewers of their god-like omniscience and of the normative distance that follows from viewers' coevality with God (to speak in the language of Metzian understanding of realist films), this unbridled voyeurism is disrupted. The viewer is no longer immune to the guilt otherwise registered in their minds because of their status as peeping-toms. The lack of realism brings the pleasure-deriving tendencies operating in the audience minds to a halt. Now shame is entailed when, caught peeping becomes the predominant feeling. For both the hero in the screen and the neighbours in the hall relay looks at each other. For, viewer is caught in the crossfire of looks and new consciousness, politically active and mindful of its mission in the real world, is instituted. It is through these modes (partial application of point-of-view shot and other modes which abolish the narrative distance) that a politically active and responsible Tamil person and his subjectivity is interpellated; a political man always mindful of the political struggle that he has to wage before bringing about a situation in which unrestrained production and consumption can be carried out. In a certain sense, our study, by tracing the genealogy of Tamil person will describe the trajectory along which he has moved. From the point of view of the middle caste non-Brahmin Tamil, the starting point is characterized by a self-conscious search for a space in which his economically productive activities can take place in a dignified and unfettered manner, and the ending point is marked by wholesale consumption of pleasure, as if the political struggle has drawn to a glorious end. We can even qualify this transition as a movement from unpleasure to pleasure; from work to play; or still more generally, from event to spectacle.

Keeping this model in mind, our analysis of films and the nature of subjectivity that they aspire to constitute in the viewers, will endeavour to appreciate the relation between cinematic medium and the socio-economic transformations that have occurred in the past few decades. But before undertaking such a textual analysis of select films belonging to each era it behooves us to give a brief account of the political history of Tamil Nadu.

The Tamil political actor, which the Dravidian movements envisioned, was a 'chauvinist' producer whose conception of work (economically productive labour) was tied closely with his struggle for an autonomous sovereign region in which his economic activities can happen. The pre-independent Dravidian movement had an avowed goal of securing a separate territory within which productive relations can be organized on their own terms, free from an overarching political entity like the Indian nation-state, which was dubbed as an expression of Brahminism. In post-independent India, even when the DMK reconciled to the compulsion to exist within the ambit of the Indian nation-state, it continued to press its claim for complete state autonomy (Manila Suyatchi) so as to reduce to a minimum the role of Indian state in determining and influencing the life circumstances of Tamil. Although these claims and protests were couched in cultural terms like imposition of Hindi on Tamils etc., the general concern beneath them was to ensure an unconstrained economic growth of Tamil middle caste and class members who were part of the Dravidian movement. This was so, because the Indian nation-state's presence was seen as nullifying their efforts, for it was allegedly siding with north Indian entrepreneurs and other outsider aspirants. The preponderance of prosperous Marwaries, and other north-Indian mercantile communities in Tamil Nadu came in handy for those who leveled this accusation.

The coincided with a general feeling of being alien in the north-Indian territory and a sense of outsiderness, which prevailed in the minds of Tamils, when being in north-India. Tamils internal resistance to learning Hindi even while operating within north-Indian zones contributed more to their lack of oneness with the pan-Indian nationalist imagination. This was further exacerbated by the absence of Tamils presence in what Benedict Anderson identified as the medium of paramount importance for the creation of national imagination, namely, print commodities. As many Tamil Congress nationalist lamented time and again , the general elision of Tamils' contribution, if any, to the Indian national struggle in nationalist historiographic records and in other forms of nationalist political discourse, had led to a situation wherein Tamils were viewed by north-Indians, at worst, as unpatriotic, particularly in relation to the national independence movement (Ramasamy 1994:320). On the other hand, within the territory of Tamil Nadu, Congress party loyalists' attempts to ally themselves with the national liberation struggle had to constantly confront the issue of not alienating themselves from the general Tamil populace which looked upon Congress as serving the interest of upper castes. It may be interesting to note here that even Tamil Muslims, during the pre-independent days joined in large number the non-Brahmin Dravidian movement in Tamil Nadu and not Congress which they dubbed as Hindu-upper-caste party (see More: 1993). Hence, Tamil's integration within the Pan-Indian national consciousness remained largely unaccomplished during the pre-independence days as well as during the next decades following independence.

Paradoxically the successive attempts made in the early 1970's in inscribing Tamils presence on the body of pre-independent national history, had been initiated by the D.M.K itself, a party whose parent organization advocated secession from the Indian state before independence. Here again we must to be careful not to read off these claims of Tamil's participation in the national liberation struggle as a grand merger of the Tamil political imaginary, with its specific sense of Tamilness and uniquely independent non-Aryan genealogy, with the blanket notion called Indianness. What underlay their overwriting of Indian history with Tamil participation duly mentioned in it, was clearly a process of localizing the national history (Ibid). The political imperative that Tamil Nadu had to exist within the Indian union and the latter's dominating presence, needed a reconstitution of the Tamil political imaginary. Even when the political imaginary of Tamils had been recast, it had to be done in Tamils own terms. This is why many forgotten Tamil leaders, whose contribution to the national independent struggle, was resurrected around this time. In contrast to this, little effort was made to make, national leaders of non-Tamil origin, part of the Tamil political pantheon (see Sumathy: 1994, for a discussion of DMK's efforts to highlight 'Kattapomman' (a folk hero) as a nationalist warrior). Therefore, it was natural that Tamils felt like outsiders in north-India, and reciprocally, north Indians viewed them as outsiders. This trend continued in one form or another till the late 1980s.

## *The Emergence of Pan-Indianism among Tamil Middle Castes:*

The present decade is politically very decisive for the state of Tamil Nadu. It is during those periods that we bear witness to a radical shift in the political imaginary of Tamils, caused by few significant events whose political implications are deeply felt by Tamils. At the dawn of this decade, June 1990 to be exact, when the ADMK, this time led by Jayalalitha, a Brahmin lady by birth, come to form the government after a landslide victory in the assembly election, it signaled the changing course of Tamil political history. This was, to be sure, a crucial index of the changing political consciousness of Tamil people. Even though her victory owed much to the sympathy wave generated by Rajiv Gandhi's assassination during the previous regime headed by the DMK, it also marks the arrival of new Tamil person whose political imaginary was characterized by a monumental guilt complex created by Rajiv Gandhi's assassination on Tamil soil on the one hand and by a new hope instilled by the implementation of Mandal Commission recommendation by the V.P.Singh Government at the center around the same time on the other hand. However, the shift in the political consciousness received its strongest impetus when the liberalization of

Indian economy was initiated by subsequent central governments. These events undermined the politics of Tamil nationalism pursued by the DMK and shared by many middle caste Tamils (see Geetha and Raja Durai, 1991:1591). More importantly the subsequent developments inspired by these events, portended an emerging politics of pan-Hindu nationalism, sponsored by Hindu upper caste elites, who found their able allies in middle caste, economically affluent Tamils, particularly Chettiyars Vellalas, Nadars, and Gounders. Ironically the same castes, which were the primary benefactors of the Dravidian movement from its inception to the late 1980's became its nemesis, as well as when they shed their commitments to the politics of Tamil nationalism. These non-Brahmin elites, who had till then cleverly exploited the political benefits accruing to them by their participation in the Dravidian politics, and thereby gained on economic ascendancy. Since the opportunities available within the territory of Tamil Nadu became saturated, these elites readied themselves to stake a moral claim over national resources. These elites now realized that their old commitment to the cultural nationalism advocated by the Dravidian parties, particularly of the DMK brand, was at odds with their desire for further expansion of their economic activities. Hence, they have now drifted towards the Hindu right, to facilitate easy entry into zones where they can make good purchase of national resources—i.e., both employment and business level resources.

If the privileged among the Tamil middle castes are joining the chorus for pan-Indian identity, and beginning to express their desire for confluencing with broad Hindu-upper-caste-defined national mainstream, it only points up a general trend perceivable at the national level, heralded by the liberalization of Indian economy and by the Mandal phenomenon. This is not surprising for it only suggests the common practice found among many ambitious young generation Indians and their current engagement with contestation of existing forms of conceiving one's national identity. This is brilliantly analysed by Satish Deshpande. He describes the disappearance of a Nehuruvian model of the Indian citizen, who is a producer-patriot and the arrival of sovereign consumer unconstrained by any nationality or communitarian identity (Deshpandey: 1993 29-30). In their drive to jump on the bandwagon of globalization, the middle class (and middle castes in Tamil context) in India are finding their old loyalties and traditional labels as constricting.

In common with the globalised middle class, Tamil middle castes have begun to regard their old conception of Tamilness either as dispensable or as pliable, thus capable of being modified to suit their larger economic goals. It is only in this context that one can understand the abrupt appearance of many pan-Indian patriot heroes in the post-liberalisation Tamil films about which we have spoken at some length in the previous section.

If middle caste elites in Tamil Nadu have taken to a pan-Hindu identity and to the neo-Brahminism professed by the BJP, it has seriously dented Tamil nationalist-tinged politics propagated by the DMK. There is no better proof to this than the process of the Dravidian politics, unleashed by Jayalalitha during her regime. Throwing, as her detractors have argued, the political philosophy and the values of the Dravidian movement to the winds Jayalalitha went on to introduce practices which are anathema to the Dravidian political culture: untrammeled eulogisation of political leaders, series of temple renovation, opening of Hindu scripture schools for all sections of Tamils are examples of this. However, the 'kitsch' politics offered by Jayalalitha failed to satisfy the self-aggrandizing middle and upper castes in Tamil Nadu. For these castes, the Tamil subject as a fighter for a dignified politico-economic Tamil space has exhausted its possibilities. Displacing the subject-as-producer is the subject-as-consumer. The Dravidian movement has achieved its aims, the economic ascendancy of Tamil middle castes. What remains to be done is the tapping of national resources on the one hand and the enjoyment of the fruits of the Dravidian movement of the other hand.

## *From Denial of Pleasure to Plentitude of Pleasure*

In the light of the political and social conditions of the post-liberalisation phase of Indian history in general and Tamils history in particular, it will be highly significant to see how films in Tamil Nadu react to these developments. We have maintained throughout this study that popular films in Tamil Nadu have been highly politicized so much so that it has displaced other modes of addressing the public. We have been in chapter 2 as to how the Dravidian movement and the political parties associated with it used film medium to constitute the psyche of viewers as potential political actors. In keeping with this thesis, we will take our analysis a step further and inquire into the political character of the post-liberalisation film. It goes without saying that post-liberalisation films, as made clear in the first section of this chapter, evince a strong tendency to efface Tamil specific references from the filmic text in accordance with the changing contours of the market. But this says little of the new subjectivity that these films constitute.

If political films of the pre-liberalisation phase cared little for the ideology of realism and gleefully employed anti-realist conventions - here one thinks of 'Manohara', 'Parasakthi', 'Nadodimannan' and 'Rickshawkkaran' to name a few - they, more than anything else, aimed at propagating a political message, thereby activating the political consciousness of the viewers, enjoining them to reflect upon their political and moral responsibilities as Tamils. Their unselfconscious deployment of direct address and positioning of the image of hero in pure frontal pose, and their scant regard for relaying the look of the character looking off-screen twice, all contributed towards making film-watching a political event, a consciously-chosen political practice. Many DMK followers went to watch these films not so much to extract voyeuristic pleasure, because there was none, but rather to learn a political lesson, to obtain designs for living their real political lives. They remained as self-reflexive political actors both in the darkened, cloistered ambience of cinema halls and in the outside world. The desire for jouissance was repeatedly muted by the so-called anti-realist techniques. Their consumerist intent must need be repressed, if political action acquires primacy. As constituting a moral community of Tamils became the avowed goal of the earlier movements, the popular view that films atomize the audiences into individual consumers, was clearly negated by these early politically motivated films.

During the early pre-liberalisation days, films in Tamil Nadu films were purely metonymical exercises. More often than not these political films transformed the iconic character of the images into indexical signs rendering the images contiguous with real life-circumstances of the Tamil people. How this happens has already been elaborated in the previous chapter. Yet we will throw light on the processes by which pleasure was denied to the audience, as a result of abolition and reduction in the narrative distance.

An pertinent point of departure for such an inquiry would be the Metzian understanding of cinema as an institution, which activates desire. This is not without significance, since cinema as a modern institution accompanied the development of capitalism and concomitant arrival of consumerism, which is reliant on the mobilization of desire. So, cinema fits in the capitalist regime by transforming itself into a commodity, which could be exchanged for money (Metz 1986: 260). The ontological significance of this transformation is what Metz called "the missed encounter" between the producer and consumer (Ibid: 262-63). The logic of capitalism introduces money as the intervening moment, thus freeing the producer from the locations of market and consumption. This paves the way for derivation of pleasure in the absence of vigilant surveillance of the produces. Similarly, the very absence of the actors (whose 'effigies' only are present on the screen) as flesh and blood beings heralds unrestrained voyeurism, for the consumer is inoculated against possible objections raised by the actors. The 'missed encounter' between the actors who are gone, by the time the consumer/spectator enters the scene of viewing is the bedrock of textual economy of cinema. The technical expression of this logic is the rendering of film into a spectacle through the evolution of certain injunctions governing the art of film-making. The set of injunctions and sanctions includes strict avoidance of direct address, depthless frontality and partial application of point-of-view and reverse shot structures. Just as the row of foot-lights marks off the theatrical space from the audience in theatre, it is through these conventions that cinematic illusion is created. It is through the affirmation and establishment of narrative distance that certain kind shamefaced voyeurism is fostered - 'shamefaced' because objects/actors in the screen are not complicit with the voyeuristic practice as, e.g., in the case of striptease act.

There is another facet to this. The enjoyment of all perceiving gaze which cinema makes available to the spectator, who can see things happening in different times and spaces without actually moving himself, quite apart from producing a shamefaced cinematic voyeur, throws the viewer away from the spectacle and seats him besides the morally and intellectually detached God himself. The moral and intellectual vantage point reserved only for God who watches the events in the world without committing Himself morally to them accrues to the spectator/consumer, whose normative standards are set by hedonist ethics of a capitalist society. For a consuming subject, somebody's agony and pain are a spectacle to be watched and enjoyed but not to be shared. For one thing, his orgasm-tinged grin and pleasure-induced giggle will not be noticed by the objects/ actors falling within this scopic regime, because of the 'missed encounter'. That cinema guided by realist aesthetics keeps the viewer at many removes away from the happenings, qualifies its status as organizer and distributor of pleasure, devoid of moral responsibilities attendant on it. After all, fantasizing about robbing a bank hardly leaves the fantasiser guilt-ridden.

What if the invisible barrier between the viewer and viewed is destroyed? What if the spectator is sucked into the narrative and finds himself in the midst of the images (which are otherwise meant for consumption), which relay their looks onto him recognizing him as a participant, by eliciting from him a morally responsible reaction? These questions are addressed in the following pages.

It is our contention that the Dravidian films of the early days, the 1950's and 1960's, smack of anti-realist tendencies; to say this is not to assert that they assumed this stand self-consciously. For it was adopted largely by default. The overturning of cinema of Metzian variety, by the antirealist posture expressing itself in the form of recurring use of direct view, by refusing to annul the threat posed by absent images and by refusing to grant the transcendental omni vision available otherwise to the spectating subject. Instead of sustaining the missed encounter, they bring the viewer and viewed face to face with each other, staring into each other eyes, generating tragic sense of being constantly caught peering at each other. The image on the screen, even its trace, looking back at the spectating obligation-reminding God. It is not the spectator who experiences the joy of being seated far away from the event at a vantage position, instead it is the images, which enjoy this godlike status. Yet, significantly, the godliness of the image is subject to perennial supervision by the viewer, as the images are aware that they are being at once 'looked at' and 'looking'. Not only is the complicity of the image annihilated with direct address and frontality positioning the image, but dismissal of voyeurism as well. Put differently, both exhibitionism of the image and voyeurism of the viewer cease to function as primary psychological tendencies. What comes to occupy the place of a subject, goaded by desire is a subject, which is part of a moral and political community with a sense of responsibility for action.

Let us demonstrate as to how the Dravidian films aspired to instigate action and engineered a direct encounter between viewer and viewed by confronting three important features which Metz listed for production and circulation of desire and pleasure in cinema, in his seminal article "The imaginary signifier". (Metz 1975: 262-278). The following arguments will highlight the Tamil-specific tendencies which undercut the psychological effect of cinema as an institution which develops it into a forum for political action. In elaborating on these tendencies, we may refute the historical and universal applicability the Metzian understanding of cinema seeks for the psychoanalytic understanding of cinema. The three features Metz identified are (1) the solitude of the spectator that is, that the spectator sits in darkness before a lit screen, making for an inevitable key hole effect (2) The complicity and ignorance of the actors in the film towards the member of audience. The actor necessarily remains in ignorance of the spectator and (3) The closeness yet inaccessibility of the place in which the unfolding of the film happens. The fantasy-world of the film, which is definitely inaccessible yet close (Metz 1975:264).

## *Incomplete Viewing-Contexts and Their Constituting A Community of Viewers:*

In elucidating our refutation of the first condition, we may remind ourselves of a caveat introduced by Andrew Higson (1990). He warns us, in one of his essays on national cinema, that any attempt to understand national cinemas independent of the 'inward looking' processes will be futile. He means those aspects related to national economy, culture and tradition. He also recommends the interrogation of national cinema in relation to the questions concerning distribution, exhibition, audience, consumption and performative contexts (Higson 1990: 39-41). Keeping this in view, let us examine the first feature of cinema by analyzing the specific contexts in which film-watching in Tamil society occurred in the early days. Contrary to the western assumption that films are watched in darkened halls where the cinematic narrative unfolds in a continuous fashion, in absolute solitude of individual viewer, it should be stated that the viewing context in Tamil Nadu was highly varied and the majority of the viewers did not enjoy the luxury of darkness in their viewing experience. The non-commercial contexts such as temple festivals, village fairs and exhibition grounds at which film-watching occurred in large measure, even now tends to reduce the viewing experience to a collective exercise. The well-lit surroundings and regular interruption because of the single projector being used keep the viewer in constant touch with reality, quite apart from creating an awareness about the community of viewers whose solidity cannot be wished away as the lighting around these viewing spaces brought into relief the presence of others around a viewer. The majority of those who lived in rural areas were subject to these experiences, as film-watching in their lives transpired equally, if not more, in non-commercial contexts. Even when it happened in commercial contexts, particularly, touring talkies were abundant then, the lack of technological sophistication (they also had one projector facility) made "reality-testing" (to borrow Walter Benjamin's phrase) possible more often than enough to make film-viewing a discontinuous experience. The frequent transporting of the viewer into the real world, forced the viewer into an eternal awareness of the community of viewers. This compelled them to hold back the voyeurs inside the viewers. Withholding of the voyeur in the viewer was further precipitated by the traditional Hindu notion of "viewing" and "looking".

Diana Eck (1981) and Lawrence Babb (1981) in their writings on 'glancing' and 'looking' and 'being looked at' (Darsan dena and darsan lena) offer interesting insights regarding the importance of "looking" in Indian culture. Many of their conclusions apply to Tamil society too. The centrality of looking in the mythico/poetic structure of Tamil society has significant effect on all spheres of life. In the religious life of Tamils, the summation of human-divine interaction is reached when reciprocal glancing between god and devotee occurs. Its most striking expression is manifest in the invocatory hymns sung by Tamil Saints belonging to Bhakti Cults. In these hymns, the devout bhaktas invoke the blessings of Lord Shiva, by entreating Him to look at them at least from the corner of his eye (Kadaikanparvai), in the ancient poems concerning the exterior/puram (war and politics) and interior/Akam (love and romance) (ref.Ramanujan) the power of looking is elaborated. In Kampan's 'Ramayana', a lengthy note is found on the exchange of glances between Raman and Seetha. Many court poets in the ancient Tamil society have waxed lyrical over the beautiful and graceful look of the king, the patron. What all these suggest is that 'looking' is equally a recognition of each one's position (devotee and divine, lover and beloved, patron and client) and more importantly of the responsibility accompanying the position. Crucial also is the non-terminal nature of 'looking'. It is not an end in itself, seeing the divine being is incomplete without being seen, and to sustain the auspiciousness accruing to viewer (because of being looked at by the divine image), the devoted should strive hard to do good deeds, to ensure that he deserves another benevolent look from God. Seen this way, the act of seeing is just the first act in the circuit of continually relayed looks between the seeing and seen. It is this notion that underpins film watching as a socio-political practice in Tamil society. In a socio-cultural set-up where conventions assert the importance of seeing as a first act, a means to an end (be it salvation or recognition of hierarchy) in a transaction, looking and being looked at, automatically results in conferring a status of an arbiter capable of passing judgments and acting upon them.

What happens when viewers carry these notions of 'viewing' and 'looking' onto film-viewing contexts where the co-presence of other viewers (other Darsan-seekers) are rendered visible because of the abundance of non-commercial contexts? It ends up transforming the space of film-reception into a politico/religious space where viewers are participants in a religious activity or in a political event.

This cultural expectation of the viewers and the socio-political behaviours and attitudes that the viewers have reserved for these contexts are duly complemented by techniques that render off-screen space contiguous to the real space of reception, like direct address, frontal stasis and incomplete application of point-of-view structure. This accounts for the participatory and interactive nature of movie viewing. The direct visual address of the images on the screen to the audience is religiously misrecognized for the divine glance and it produces a prohibitive and instigative effect. Thus, many devotional films excite viewers to such an extent that women spectators suddenly break into ecstatic possession dance on seeing their favourite God/Goddess[3] (See Veena Das, 1985).

An expression of the reciprocal awareness, of viewer and viewed and their mutual interaction is seen in the film 'Annamalai' (1993). This film is a Rajinikanth starrer, in which, during a song sequence, Rajinikanth abruptly looks out of the screen at the audiences and throws a question at them, the answer to which is supposed to rhyme with the last word mentioned before the question. Using the mode of frontal address, he confidently assumed the fact that audience has answered his question and nods his head in approval and appreciation of the received answer, which invariably comes from staunch sans of Rajinikanth sitting in the hall. Though it may seem a stark violation of classical realist aesthetics, it is not ill-suited to the interpretive regime peculiar to Tamil audience. Neither the actor nor the viewer, as this example indicates, remains ignorance of each other being there.

The previous chapter, showed through a Dravidian film, 'Manohara, how the iconic nature of the image of hero is transposed into an indexical sign, to elicit consensus from the audience for the DMK's political culture agenda. This holds true in the present context of our analysis of desire and its denial in pre-liberalisation films. To this, we may add the following. The mutation of hero's image into an indexical sign so as to collapse the off-screen space of film into actual-space of viewing and beyond, was accomplished not only through application of certain anti-realist camera conventions and editing (which was non-continuous) but also through selective incorporation of details, such as the choice of names, epithets like 'self-respect' valour (veeram); 'rationality' (Pakutharivu) etc., and biographical and actual situations common to both viewers and actors. These modes refused to grant a moral vantagepoint to the viewer and kept them orbiting within the wheels of narrative. The rejection of pleasure-entailing[4] processes and details in films was clearly manifest in the very choice of locations and landscapes. While 'Manohara', strictly parries elaboration of scenes that would present themselves for enjoyment.

## *An Invitation to Consumers*

The Elicitation of New Attitudes in Post-Liberalisation Films.In our critique of the universalizing and generalizing import of Metzian understanding of cinema as an edifice erected on the notion of desire, we made, albeit implicitly, a case for taking due recognizance of the actual infrastructural details of film-viewing contexts, particularly their hard-ware. If the production of pleasure depends, as it does, on the specular effect of the image's spatial institutionalisation, it necessitates perfect reception spaces which ensures faithful uninterrupted reproduction of images, leave alone the importance of realistic framing and editing or pro-filmic material including the actors. This, when lacking, mightily upset the operation the two fundamental sexual drives on which cinema relies. They are 'scopohilia' the desire to see and what Lacan referred to as 'invocatory drive', the desire to hear. Hence, when any effort is made to posit cinema as a desire-producing institution, one should not lose sight of the actual development of architectural aspect of the institution. History of cinema must, of necessity, be juxtaposed to history of material resources and infrastructural facilities specific to the viewing contexts, if a complete understanding is sought. Conceived in this way, the real moment of arrival of a capitalist-consumer whose confidence in encountering the absent ones (the missed encounter) is inaugurated by two developments; one 'gentrification' and improvement of viewing contexts, viz., cinema halls; and the other, the wholesale and loyal adoption of the ideology of realism in capturing the pro-filmic events and materials. The former makes sure that the scopophilic and invocatory drives are catered to in the viewing contexts. Whereas the latter perfectly complements it by assuring the 'definitely inaccessible elsewhereness' of the event on the screen. These developments reinstate a morally detached intellectually-distanced, transcendental sovereign consumer, for whom seeing is an end in itself, the first and last act (seeing is believing", the motto of cinema as it emerged in the modern west). If the pre-liberalisation Tamil commercial films' rejection of the aesthetics of realism, compounded further by preponderance of non-commercial, "ill-suited," viewing-contexts, sought to convey to the viewers a sense of loss, lack, and crisis, by positioning the images within a non-realistic perceptual field, continuously flowing out onto the real space to suck the viewer into itself, the imposition of realist aesthetics and the corresponding sophistication of the hardware, rendered the events conveying crisis into a spectacle. If the former obliged the viewers to share the images of crisis and moments of anxieties, the latter encouraged them to enjoy and consume the very images of crisis in a dispassionate manner.

If one carefully traces the architectural and architectonic history of cinematic institution to Tamil Nadu, one can perhaps mark the above-mentioned developments reaching its saturation point around the late 1980's. Both viewing contexts and the application of the aesthetics of realism were perfected at this time. Yet this is merely so for the dominant trend, for films that discard realist canons continue to be made even in the nineties.

It is around this period, that the pre-conditions for the advent of realistic cinema (cinema in the Metzian sense) were fulfilled. This, in turn, created the opportunity for the entry of the Tamil-middle class subject who has been given the material wherewithal by the Dravidian movement to become a consumer of leisure. Thus, there has been a large-scale influx of young, urbane, cosmopolitan-looking film artists who are the beneficiaries of the Dravidian movement whose relevance was dimmed by the time these artists arrived in Tamil cinema (they are third generation Tamils after the birth of the Dravidian movement). It is this generation that is excited about the prospect of becoming a globalised middle class, hankering for resources and pleasures available both at the national and transnational levels... It is this generation which has vested interest in celebrating the birth of a new subject and a cosmopolitan imagination. For them, old symbols and metaphors suggestive of old loyalties, old form of political alignments tempered with Tamil cultural nationalism, ceased to be profitable and meaningful. True to our goal set out in this study let us try to discern how these tendencies are visible in post-liberalisation films like 'Roja', 'Bombay' and 'Indian'. The nature of subjectivity sought to be normalized for the Tamils and choice of filmic strategies to achieve this will concern us in the next section.

## *SPECTACULARISATION OF CINEMA AND THE CONSTITUTION OF DESIRENG SUBJECT*

In what follows we shall briefly touch upon some of the tendencies, indicative of the changing modes through which a new conception of self-hood is being instituted in the minds of Tamils by these post-liberalisation commercial films. These tendencies need to be examined and described, through a rigorous reading of these films.

The increasing sophistication of film-making technologies and materials -- better quality films, color processing etc., which enable the film-makers to claim a status of verisimilitude to their cinematographic practices, combines handsomely with perfected viewing contexts, equipped with digital, multi-track sound systems, high-tech projection facilities, cozy in-theatre features so on and so forth. This is further augmented by innovations introduced in filmmaking processes themselves.

This is best exemplified by the incorporation of seductive advertisement formulas into film-making. The ideology of advertisement as a normalizing agency of desire cannot be overestimated. The twin-aspect of a mass-produced economy, namely, the emergence of consumer society and the need to increase the quantum of 'wants' call for advertisement as a means to further them, need also to be taken into account. "Advertising naturalizes the mysterious 'life of thing' and affirms it as the source of all positive human attributes. Consumption in this situation is a means of achieving identity, a project of self-definition using socially approved meaning "(Rajagopal 1994:1661). The deployment of ad-film making conventions in feature film-making have now become so common among film-makers. This is so not only because of the large-scale entry of ad-film technicians into film-making, but also necessitated by the need to sell off the film in the market well before the movie reaches completion.

Film as a pure commodity and film-watching as a buyable experience set films in competition with other commodities created for enjoyment—one may recall here theme parks, travel and tourism, holidaying etc. Thus, filmmakers are goaded to convert their films simultaneously into full-length advertisement, which is becoming increasingly self-referential in nature. This is very crucial. The film promotional pieces we watch on TV, with its split-screen and multiple-image in one single frame are presented as if they are mere moving wallposters. This is not different from the way film songs—the veritable index of the richness, grandeur, newness etc. of the movies are picturized.

That movies are at once self-referring advertisements, techniques of the latter tend to get employed on a significant scale in films, explains the influx of ad-film makers into commercial films. Leading from the front in this respect is Mani Ratnam whose film 'Roja' exploited the favorable environment created by economic liberalization[5] and globalization. The songs in his films are shot on elaborates sets using catchy advertisement techniques assisted by cute teeny-bopper tunes composed by A.R.Rahman, an erstwhile jingle musician. The essential recipes for ad-films like fast cutting, a semi-autonomous theme, pre-fabricated location etc. are also found in his film songs. Following Mani Ratnam's success many new-generation film-directors, cameramen, art-directors and others, all having had a stint in advertisement-making entered the film world. In this regard the opening of film-city in Madras could not have been better timed. This gave an opportunity to the film-makers to virtually create any kind of ambience, which can be fabricated to the last detail. This helped enhance the cosmopolitan tenor of these films such that they might fit into any cultural setting. This accounts for the deterritorialised and de-ethicised look of these films. 'Roja', 'Kadhal Desam', 'Minsara Kanavu', all fall under this category. This apart, the spectacular presentation of eye-catching landscapes, elaboration of carefully-chosen rural and idyllic, urban locations and exotic images of foreign countries qualify these films as scenic post-cards made mobile, so to speak. They are meant to activate the desires of the emerging social type, tourist-friendly destinations, both domestic and foreign, acquires further fillip through these films. Small wonder that some of these films are capable of passing off as tourism-department documentaries. If pre-liberalisation films depicted conflict-ridden zones teeming with villainous treacherous images, scaring the viewers off these places, the post-liberalisation films in the like of 'Minsara Kanavu' (the director of this film Rajiv Menon called the film a feel-good and enjoyable film) present a narrative world devoid of villains, thus viewer (read tourist) friendly.

We have tried, in the passages above, only a tentative description of dominant and upcoming trends. Interestingly these seductive films - villainless, pure scenic, ad-like—are paralleled by films still incorporating anti-realist conventions on a massive scale. Here one may mention several of Rajinikanth's films. The excessive use of unmotivated direct address and negligible regard for self-enclosed narrative space which fosters "elsewhereness" of a filmic event, permitting highly participative viewing both at the time of exhibition (see above) and outside of viewing context (fan clubs deciding the resolution of the conflict in the film, leave alone other minor details like the number of punches Rajinikanth should get from the baddies, the sanitized abuse which Rajinikanth should receive form villains etc.) all fly in the face of the aesthetics of realism which the feel-good filmmakers seek to impose clinically on Tamil commercial films. However, the class and caste character of the public, which patronizes the latter types of films, speak of the multiple aspiration-structures that prevail in Tamil society. If the middle caste elites declare, doubtless by their discomfiture with Rajinikanth's direct and frontal address (they look askance when Rajinikanth looks at them, they keep quite when he expects an answer) it is because the realness of the struggle that he affirms ceases to appeal to them, the economically prosperous consumerist middle castes/ classes.

## *Concluding Remarks*

What this study aspired to do was to examine the triangular relationship between politics and art form, that is cinema on the one hand and politics and culture on the other. By focusing on popular cinema, I sought to chart the changing forms of political imaginary and the political imaginary and the collective social aspiration of Tamils. This is because popular cinema, occupying a strategic place in the public cultural realm, constitutes and is constituted by the collective goals. In contrast to those studies which naively treated films as a mirror reflecting the socio-political dynamics of a given society, I have paid due attention to the ideological dimension of cinema. That is to say, because of its wider popularity and its forceful nature, cinema was/is used by many interest groups to shape and distribute opinions that may prove conducive to the realization of the goals that the interest groups want to achieve. In this study, I described the processes by which the Dravidian movements moulded the Tamil psyche, so as to ensure a constituency of supporters for their political projects.

Equally important is the fact that Tamil popular cinema is reciprocally constituted by the contesting social groups. They articulate their socio-political aspiration through available cultural media, like cinema. Thus, art forms can be taken up as reliable weathervane that may point to the vicissitudes a society undergoes. Between these two ways of considering popular cinema as a medium, which controls and is controlled by the socio-political imaginary comes the phenomenological understanding of cinema. It is with the strongly felt phenomenological sensitivity that I tried to take due cognizance of the processes by which individual viewers appropriated the cinematic medium and the meanings it generated to suit their life-situations. Through their interpretive and appropriating strategies, they enabled and empowered themselves to construct a life-world which makes sense to them. However due to the limitations specific to a small study like ours we could not go deeply into the modes of appropriation which film-going audiences in Tamil Nadu used. Yet this sensitivity runs throughout the entire study as it is obvious, for instance, from our analysis of Rajinikanth's fan's appropriation of his image and his films to register their presence in the cultural geography of Tamil society.

In keeping with the current dominant view in the cultural studies discipline, this study took full view of the fact that the consumers of the cultural media are not passive recipients. On the contrary they are active participants. In the whole process of consuming a cultural product, the consumer constructs meanings in stark contrast to the ones intended by the produce, contests the meanings intended and encodes different meaning he finds suitable to his life situation. When engaging in the act of consumption the consumer carries with himself a whole repertoire of notions, information and experiences specific to his life world. Right through our study we paid enough attention to these tendencies and have attempted to understand film-watching in Tamil Nadu in the environment of symbols, and culture-specific notions and practices.

In fine, this study must be regarded as modest endeavour to construct the archeology of the Tamil political imaginary and the genealogy of the Tamil middle caste person through the eyes of an active member of Tamil society, who looks at his own self from a distance, as it were. In this regard this may, at best, be treated as a personalized account of the history of Tamil middle caste psyche. With skills necessary to study a society as removed from it as possible and with the sentiments and personalised experiences sufficient to feel intrigued by the changes unleased by recent socio-processes at national and international level, the researcher has written a sociological autobiography tempered duly with the philosophies of social scientific research.

---

End Notes

[1] We have already talked about the twice-relayed nature of the character's look completing the point-of-view structure, along Metzian line. William Rothman following Metz suggests the following description. The three-shot structure which is the general Hollywood norm, has three sequence: First the character looking, then what is seen, and then the character's look again. This is a complete structure but when the same three-shot structure is applied incompletely, it tends to throw open the cinematic event, for direct encounter with the viewers who throng the off-screen space instead of the looking character (Rothman 1993). In a Rajinikanth starrer 'Muthu' (1995) a sequence happens suggesting something similar. When the Comedian inquires Rajinikanth's mother about Rajini's whereabouts, she says "he must be now riding his chariot as fast as he used to...." As she begins to visualize the event through her mind's eye, we get to see a song sequence, full of political messages, in which he rides his chariot. But the end of song does not result with our relayed look (relayed through the hero's mother's mind's eye) returning to the mother figure, in lieu of that we notice that the film proceeds from his returning home on his chariot, rendering the song sequence a pure spectacle presented only for the off-screen audience in the theater.

[2] Agreeing with Jokbson's understanding of metaphor we define the former as a literary device by which a thing or even is made to represent r convey the meaning specific to a whole or another independent thing because of these two sets being associated with each other by principle of contiguity, e.g., stockings of a lady representing the lady herself. Metaphor, on the other hand, is a literary device by which two independent objects and events share the same meaning because of their apparent similarity, e.g., a toy representing a woman because of similar looks.

[3] It may interest us to note that many cine halls in urban parts of Tamil Nadu (including small towns) have features redolent of Hindu temples. It may range from temple-like interior decoration, lighting arrangement, the

choice of name given to theatres, male-female division, to devotional songs played before the film-show begins.

[5] It is said that Mani Ratnam's brother, a well –known film-producer G.Venkatesan, floated the shares for this film in the capital market to mobilize money for it.

CHAPTER FIVE

# FILM SONGS, FILM AND TAMIL PUBLIC: TAKING STOCK OF THEIR CHANGING RELATIONSHIP

In this chapter a critical approach to the widely-held notion of genius and to the question of genre- development is advanced in the context of radical paradigm shift witnessed in the history of film music in Tamil Nadu. Also inquired are the structure of the relationship between film songs and films on the one hand and film songs and Tamil public on the other. A sociological understanding of artwork like music can ill-afford to elide the process of social construction of artworks and, by implication, their popularity.

For the purpose of clarity, I would like to situate the arguments of this chapter, in the midst of recurring debates raging over the 'organic nature" of the music of Ilaiyaraja, who virtually monopolized film music in Tamil Nadu for nearly four decades and the "kitsch" music of A.R.Rahman whose all-India popularity needs little introduction. While the generation that grew up with Ilayaraja's music is busy criticizing the 'jingle -like' music of Rahman, the new-generation is totally wowed by brand-new sounds and timbre that Rahman is dishing out in his music. However, I am less concerned here with the personality of musicians per se and more with the issue of sociological determinants of cultural taste. Indeed, the question of genius of either of these musicians cannot be detached from the socio-cultural experiences of the respective audience these musicians command respect from. What I aspire to do here is to wade through the personalities of these musicians to throw light on the sociological and technological pre-conditions that prepared the ground for the advent of these musicians and their diverse approaches to film-music.

I basically see both these musicians as the products of specific historical circumstances that prevailed during their arrival. This is not to make little of their inherent talents. Take the case of the music of A.R.Rahman. The all-India popularity that he achieved during the last few years is the outcome of careful disavowal of an organic tie to any particular culture or tradition (which, as a matter of fact, becomes a disadvantage). Moreover the increasing urbanization of Tamils in particular and Indians in general and the cosmopolitan experience that it entails, create a situation in which homesickness (read, nostalgic yearning for a coherent tradition and singular past) become a burden and liability. Hence the cultural taste that inheres them tends to be uncomfortable with any artwork that is embedded deeply in a tradition. If Rahman's music begins with Egyptian crooning followed by African drumbeats and ends with Malayali folk tune in the background of Carnatic instrumental music, it shows as much the expanding nature of the Tamil and Indian public as it shows the expanding but superficial knowledge of these many musical tradition on the part of metropolitan citizens in India. The emergence of Rahman coincides with the triumph of metropolitan cultural superegos in determining the success and reach of popular cultural forms. This goes well with the throwaway society (a la Alvin Toffler) that is beginning to emerge in the urban centres of India in which the turnover time of an item has a shortened life span waiting to be discarded at the moment of the arrival of a new item that immediately supersedes the old one. The urban Indian's over-saturated -with-information environment looks for shocking messages to catch the attention of the people, since attention is the scarcest resource there. In these circumstances that which is new and possesses maximal impact by virtue of its new sounds and timbre (as in the case of Rahman's music) that receives admiration. In these urban centres people from all cultural centres have come to live together and their culture is a mélange of all diverse tradition. Rahman's music is cosmopolitan music which immediately appeals to these people in the cosmopolitan centres in which identification with one particular tradition is a risk one avoids. In like manner, Rahman's music does not acknowledge its bond to any particular musical tradition as it may undermine its prospective popularity. This is in contrast to Ilayaraja's music which constantly drew it inspiration and vitality from a more narrowed source to which that music was ostensibly gifted back. Ilaiyaraja aimed at an audience whose lived-tradition, felt-sentiments and experienced-emotions were the sources of his inspiration. He was very happy when his music appealed to audience from across boundaries although it was a volunteered-audience rather than an aimed-audience. The very qualities that provided the base for Ilayaraja 's music are now dispensed with for fear of losing a fast-expanding market. But this is not to make a saint of Ilaiyaraja, for he belonged to a different era.

Around 1970's when Ilaiyaraja was becoming a popular musician, there was a significant technological change that coincided with the changing demographic pattern in Tamil Nadu. It was also around this time a new generation of urbanites was born. This was a generation whose ties with rural areas were beginning to be weakened even though not fully severed. As a result of monetization of agro-economy and the new-found hope in the non -brahmin movement's promise of upward mobility, the middle castes were attracted from villages to towns. While the generation that migrated to towns and cities had already spent their formative periods in rural areas, the next generation that followed was thoroughly city-bred with village ties still intact. And Ilaiyaraja himself belonged to this generation which is partly rural and partly urban. His experience in the rural milieu blended with his adulthood spent in westernized cities. The sound that his music produced approximated and captured this blend making it appealing to the generation for which he himself stood as a specimen. In this task he was duly aided by the technological development that occurred around that time . Widespread use of tape recorders and gramophone on the one hand, and the extensive reach of radio Ceylon (Sri Lankan broadcasting corporation's Tamil language broadcast) on the other hand made film-music listening a predominant entertainment form for the ordinary masses. particularly the large scale production and the economic viability of cassette-enabled film -music to acquire excessive geographical mobility taking it to rural areas and even to neighbouring states, particularly Kerala, Andhra Pradesh. The broad-basing of the 'public' which listened to Ilaiyaraja 's music necessitated textural and structural change in it. On the other hand the flexibility and the heightened fidelity which tape cassettes offered encouraged him to introduce sounds that are irreproducible in the previous forms of storing music, namely gramophone records. This resulted not only in the blending of folk tunes, but also in the incorporation of certain pan -south Indian features in the Tamil film music, since the cassettes made marketability of both songs and films in other regions within south India a possibility.

## *The triumph of visual over auditory*

The general accusation levelled at Ilayaraja's film-music is the drowning of verbal clarity in the cacophony of sound. Yet this accusation is mild when compared to present day trend in which the visual has taken over auditory -- both in respect to verbal clarity and sound. In the context of Ilayaraja's music and its relationship film medium, it may be argued that there was certain a kind of sovereignty which film songs enjoyed, although their existence is integrated with films of which they are parts. But in the recent days, with the increasing technicalisation of film-making, film-music is fast losing its autonomy, since we witness the progressive, triumph of visual over auditory. In Ilayaraja's songs, the songs had their own independent biographies which did not require the authorship of the visual to complete their life stories. People listened to his songs as aural representation of moods and sceneries whose construction were left to the listener's creativity. Before the advent of satellite TV and cable TV songs were songs for their own intrinsic values, because it was still possible to detach the consumption of songs from the consumption of visuals specific to them. Put in other words, the independent consumption of film-songs was possible because of our not being surrounded by the visual images of these songs as it is the case now. The music director on majority of the occasions was victorious over the movie director in the past. But the communication revolution indexed by the abrupt expansion of satellite, TV, cable TV and the radical expansion of market, both at national and transnational level coupled with the need to seduce the consumer to buy a product, necessitated by stiff competition between products, have fundamentally transformed the very nature of film music in general and undercut the autonomy of film songs as primarily aural experience on the other hand. Living in a 'society of spectacle' we are increasingly being deluged of visuals and images; 'seeing' has relegated 'hearing' to the sideways of cultural experience. An incurable Freudian would have characterised this as a logical outcome, as for him the birth of ego is achieved at the moment of 'seeing' which is preceded by moments of hearing, both when the child was in the womb and immediately after its birth. But the same story has a tragic end here in the case of cultural experiences.

In a world dominated by images, every song is a piece of advertisement with a potentially higher seductive value. The success of the movie now depends upon the successful projection of its songs which build pleasure into the movie. The proliferation of music TV channels has brought about this trend.

According to the logic of these changed situations, it is the successful packaging of songs that decides the success of the movie itself. Since TV requires visual representation along with aural, and the appeal of visual is more powerful (as psychologists would have us convinced) than the aural, greater care is taken to make the song as catchy as possible. Because each song along with its visuals in a film has become a powerful advertisement, lots of money is pumped into making songs a visual extravaganza. Till recently songs revolved around the main theme of the movie, now the trend is reversed. It is around songs the theme is built in most film. This is the reason why intricate plots, twisted story lines, dramatic turnaround have vanished from the films of recent days, 'Hum Apke Hai Kaun', 'Dilwale Dulhania Le Jayenge' and 'Rangeela' are examples of that kind. Instead of looking at the arrival of light stories without a clearly-defined villain and the advent of fantasy movies from the point of view of the changing world view of the audience, we have to look at as the product of the politic al economy of liberalization of Indian market.

The emergence of visual as the dominant representation of the cultural items, be it cinema or shoes, soaps or anything that we see in TV advertisement, has damaged the autonomy of auditory, be it a song, or voiceover or dialogue in a film. Visual has imposed itself on the aural. We witness a merger of two independent biographies (specific to aural and visual) into one in which the experience of one becomes impossible without another. The merger, however, is asymmetrical since visual still takes upper hand over the auditory. For the latter's biography is written by the former, which interestingly is self-authored. The problem with this merger is the death of the creative listener, the disappearance of an aesthetically-free audience who inscribed his/her experience on the surface of the song or the piece of music which has an overarching life of its own. The imagination of the song or music ran wild and free, conditioned by nothing but his or her personal experiences. Nothing was permanently written on the body of the music except its transcendental beauty, the capturing of which becomes the spiritual quest. But when visual takes precedence over aural, ours' wonderfully vagabond imagination is tamed to think unidirectionally. The audiences lose their freedom and it heralds the end of sovereign music. It is only those who are willing to sacrifice the aural at the altar of visual who can take lightly of the present-day music genre, dominated by 'jingle like' music of today. Now song as aural experience has to cut its limbs to suit the taste of scenes. This along with the repeated showing of the song sequences in TV makes it impractical to listen to a song without trapping ourselves into the visualization of the same by the director. Along with the songs the scenes also become part of public knowledge. Both become conterminous to each other.

This is very much in keeping with the need to appeal to the expanding market boundaries that are as wide as (sometimes wider than) national boundaries. Apart from the form that the new music genre takes, the style and content are also markedly different from its predecessor. A song which becomes an icon standing for the entire movie, when shown in a satellite TV network addresses itself not only to a particular audience residing in a particular cultural sphere, but also to a multitude of audiences residing in various diasporas, in different parts of the world. The need to appeal to all these audiences does not require mastery in the specific tradition but an invention of new language which makes sense to each audience whichever place they may live in the world. The important thing in diasporas, be it Tamils in Malaysia, Sri Lanka, Gulf countries or even in Delhi, have constructed the idioms and metaphors for Tamilness or Indianness in their own way which would be different from one diaspora to another and drastically different from parent tradition. Their tradition would be a mixture of local culture with parent culture, to which they have a second-hand knowledge and accessibility only. The "puritan" nature of musical tradition would make very little sense to them. For example Indian musical tradition in Caribbean Islands is a mixture of Rap and Hindustani; that of Sri Lankan Tamils is a mixture of Sinhalese musical tradition with Tamil film-musical tradition. The simultaneous appeal to all these diasporas demands a third language which is an admixture of all unique traditions specific to each diaspora. The need to invent a third language becomes acutely necessary as the same cultural product becomes accessible to different cultural zones simultaneously, unlike in the past in which a cultural item, say film, would enter different zones. Different dimension here refers to difference in language in those cases in which a film is dubbed in to another language in or difference in plot construction in cases of remaking the same movie. However when a cultural item is aimed to reach all audiences at one given time, it has to distance itself from each tradition in such a way it appeals to all of them. In the same manner when a song is projected in the TV networks, they only initiate a process, which also involves releasing the movie simultaneously in several theatres across the world and other associated processes. In the case of western movies (this trend is soon catching up with Indian popular films) the movie is also an advertisement for movie-related merchandise which range from caps, T-shirts, shoes, toys etc. Therefore the songs in the case of Indian films play the role of an advertisement for the latter.

These processes have a negative - or a 'decisive' -- impact on the linguistic aspect of the film songs. Particularly in the cases of many Tamil films, the songs begin with non-sensical syllables which enable the songs to be immediately dubbed in to other languages without changing visuals in which the lip movement would sync with the nonsensical syllables which can be retained in other languages also, e.g. the hamma... hamma ... song in the film 'Bombay' begins with the same syllables in other languages apart from Tamil. The structural impact that becomes visible in recent days in the film songs is the autonomous plot which a song has on its own. This is in commensuration with the need to sell the film song as an independent product in its own right. The separate plot -- totally divergent from the main plot of the movie fulfils the twin purpose of selling it as a separate product and floating it as an advertisement for the movie. e.g., Mukkabla... mu quabla... in the film "Ham sai He Mquabla."

Under these circumstances music that derives its beauty and sustenance from one particular tradition is likely to have a limited appeal. They fall out of the favour of the champions of globalisation. Purity is a curse; identification with one's own tradition is not a virtue in the present circumstances. The logic of 'pastiche' succeeds. An average Indian now lives his everyday life enjoying the benefits of the luxury of object produced in different cultural zone. An average, urban Tamil's cultural milieu is filled with sounds and images which are from diverse origins from American to Africa, to West Indies to his own culture. A quick stroll in the streets of Madras would likely to fill our ears and eyes with sound images of western culture as intensely as with sound and images of north Indian and south Indian tradition. The environs around a resident of any metropolitan city are sure to have everything from everywhere rendering his/her experiences more and more cosmopolitan and synthetic. There, in these circumstances, searching for a pure tradition may not only run the danger of making oneself look buffoon-like, but making him a suspect in the eyes of others.

# Bibiliogrpahy


1. Appadurai, Arjun, et al, 1991, *Gender, Genre and powering South Asian Expressive Traditions*, University of Pensylvania Press, Philadelphia.
2. Babb, Lawerence, 1981, 'Glancing: Visual interaction in Hinduism,' *Journal of Anthropological Research*, No 37, PP 381-401.
3. Barnett, Steve, A, 1976, *Politics of Cultural nationalism in South India*, Princeton University Press, Princeton.
4. Barnett, Steve, A, 1976, 'Coconuts and Gold,' *Contributions to Indian Sociology*, No 10, PP 133-156
5. Barthes , Roland, 1985, ' *The Third meaning' in Responsibility of Forms: Critical essays on music, art and representation* (eng.tr), Basil Blackwell, London.
6. Baskaran, Theodore, 1981, *The message Bearers*, cre-A, Madras.
7. Branigan, Edward, 1985, 'Point of view Shot', in Bill Nicholas (ed) *Movies and Methods II*, University of California Press, Berkely and Los Angeles.
8. Breckendridge, Carol and Peter Van der Veer (eds), 1993, *Orientalism and Post-Colonial Predicament*, Oxford University Press, New Delhi.
9. Clothey, Fred, 1978, *The Many faces of Murukan*, Mouton Press, Hague.
10. Cohen, Abner, 1974, *Two-Dimensional Man*, Routledge and Kegan Paul, London.
11. Daniel, Valentine, 1987, *Fluid Signs: Being the Person the Tamil Way*, California University Press, Berkeley.
12. Deshpande, Satish, 1993, Imagined Economies, *Journal of Arts and Ideas*, No 25-26, December PP.5-35.
13. Dickey, Sara, 1990, Politics of Adulation, *Journal of Asian Studies*, Vol 53.
14. ,1993, *Cinema and Urban Poor in South India*, Cambridge University Press, Delhi.
15. Dudley. Andrew, 1992, History And Timelessness in Film theory and History,' in D.Klenn and William Schweiker (eds), *Meaning in Text and Action*, University Press of Virginia.
16. Geetha, V and S.V.Rajadurai, 1991, 'Dravidian Politics: End of an era, *EPW*, June 19, PP. 1951.
17. Hall, Stauart and Paul du Gay, 1996, *Cultural Identity*, Sage Publication New Delhi.
18. Hardgrave (Jr), Robert, 1979, *Essays on the Political Sociology of South*

*India,* Usha Publication, New Delhi.

19. Hardy, Fredhelm, 1983, *Viraha_Bhakthi,* Oxford University Press, New Delhi.
20. Hart III, George, 1975, 'Ancient Tamil Literature: Its scholarly past and future', in Burton Stein (ed) *Essays on South India,* University Press of Hawai.
21. Higson, Andrew, 1989, 'The concept of National Cinema', *Screen,* Vol 30, No. 4.
22. Irschick, E.F, 1969. *Politics and social conflict in South India,* University of California Press, Berkeley.
23. Kapur, Geetha, 1993 'Revelation and Doubt: Sant Tukaram and Devi,' in Tejaswani Nijanjana, et al (eds), *Interrogating Modernity,* Seagul Books.
24. Metz, Christian, 1986, Imaginary Signifier, in Philip Rosen (ed) *Narrative, Apparatus Ideology,* Columbia University Press, New York, PP. 244-78.
25. More, 1992, 'Tamil Muslims and Non-Brahmin Athesists,' *Contributions to Indian Sociology.* Vol 26
26. Oster, A, et al (eds), 1979, *Concept of Person,* Oxford University Press New Delhi.
27. Pandian, M.S.S, 1991, 'Parasakthi: Life and Times of a DMK Film,' *E P W,* Annual No., March.
28. , 1992, *The Image Trap*: Sage Publication , New Delhi.
29. ----------------, 1993, 'Denationalising the Past, '*E P W,* oct 16, P.P.2282-2287.
30. Prasad, Madhava, 1993, 'Cinema and the Desire for Modernity, '*Journal of Arts and Ideas,* No. 25-26. December
31. Radaway, Janice, 1986, 'Reading is not Eating, '*Book Research Quarterly,* Vol.2, Fall.
32. Ramanujan, A.K. and Stuart Blackburn, 1986, *Another Harmony,* Oxford University Press, New Delhi.
33. Ramasamy, Sumathi, 1994, 'The Nation, the Region and the adventures of a Tamil Hero,' *Contributions to Indian Sociology,* Vol.28, No.2, July-December, PP.2895-321.
34. -----------------, 1993, 'En/gendering Nation, '*Comparative Studies of Society and History* PP.683-723.
35. Sivathambi, Kathirkesu, 1984, *Cinema as a Medium of Political Communication in Tamil Nadu,* New Century Book House, Madras.
36. Stam, Robert, et al,1992, *New Vocabularies in Film semiotics,* Routledge &

Kegan Paul, London.

37. Trawick, Margaret, 1991, 'Wandering lost,' in Appadurai, et al, *Gender Genre and Power in South Asian Expressive traditions*, University of Pensylvania Press.
38. Valdez (ed), 1991, Ricoeur Reader: *Reflection and Imagination*, Harwest wheatshef, New York.
39. Vasudevan, Ravi, 1993, 'Shifting codes, Dissolving identities,' *Journal of Arts and Ideas*. No 23-24, October.
40. ---------, 1995, 'Film studies: New Cultural History and Experience of Modernity,' *E P W,* Vol.4.
41. -----------, 1995b, 'You cannot live in society and ignore it: Nationhood and female modernity in Andaz,' *Contributions to Indian sociology* (n.s), Vol.1-2.
42. ---------------, 1995, 'Addressing the spectator of a third world national cinema: The Bombay Social Film of the 1940s and 1950s,' *Screen,* Vol.36, No.4, winter.
43. -------------, 1991, 'The cultural space of a film narration: Interpreting Kismet,' *Contributions to Indian sociology*. Vol.28, No.2, April-June.
44. Willies, Paul, 1975, in Benthal, J and Ted Polhemus (eds), *Body as a Medium of Expression,* Allen lane, London.

www.ingramcontent.com/pod-product-compliance
Lightning Source LLC
LaVergne TN
LVHW070033160826
845671LV00009B/260

* 9 7 9 8 8 9 5 1 9 2 8 5 6 *